Michael Paterson is the author of several history books, including *A Brief History of Life in Victorian Britain*, also published by Constable & Robinson.

Recent titles in the series

A BRIEF HISTORY OF

# The Private Life of
# Elizabeth II

## MICHAEL PATERSON

ROBINSON    RUNNING PRESS
PHILADELPHIA · LONDON

To my god-daughter, Isobel Macauslan

Constable & Robinson Ltd
55–56 Russell Square
London
WC1B 4HP
www.constablerobinson.com

First published in the UK by Robinson,
an imprint of Constable & Robinson, 2011

A copy of the British Library Cataloguing in Publication
Data is available from the British Library

UK ISBN: 978-1-84901-581-3

1 3 5 7 9 10 8 6 4 2

First published in the United States in 2011 by Running Press Book Publishers,
A Member of the Perseus Books Group

Books published by Running Press are available at special discounts for bulk purchases in
the United States by corporations, institutions, and other organizations. For more information, please contact the Special Markets Department at the Perseus Books Group, 2300
Chestnut Street, Suite 200, Philadelphia, PA 19103, or call (800) 810-4145, ext. 5000, or email
special.markets@perseusbooks.com

US ISBN 978-0-7624-4279-9
US Library of Congress Control Number: 2010940977

9 8 7 6 5 4 3 2 1
Digit on the right indicates the number of this printing

Running Press Book Publishers
2300 Chestnut Street
Philadelphia, PA 19103-4371

Visit us on the web!
www.runningpress.com

# CONTENTS

I thank my wife Sarah, who by constantly asking: 'Haven't you finished that book about the Queen yet?' galvanised my efforts. I am also most grateful to some very dear friends: Jurgen and Irene Erdmann, and Astrid and Detlef Stollfuss, for most helpful conversations.

# PREFACE

She is a bit late, and you have been waiting for long minutes. A message came through that she is held up in traffic, but now there has been an announcement: 'Right, everyone! She's on her way! Places please!' and the subdued conversation ceases among your neighbours. They are standing stiffly, patiently, in a long row, not fidgeting.

You know she has arrived when you hear the sirens, faint at first, then loud enough to fill the street outside. Beyond the distant glass doors you are aware of lights flashing. There is the gunning of motorcycle engines, the crackle of police radios. And there is a flurry of movement at the entrance. Then silence. Somewhere at the far end of the receiving-line she is being greeted, talking to her hosts, having the evening's event explained to her even though she has known for more than a year that she was coming here tonight. The others, like you, are probably going over what they will say and do when they meet her. There are certain rules that have been explained: when introduced, address her first as 'Your Majesty', after that as 'Ma'am'. 'Ma'am' to rhyme with 'jam', not 'marm' as in 'marmalade'. Women may curtsy, men may bow from the neck. These gestures are not compulsory. It is, apparently, no longer necessary to make them if you prefer not to. But most still do, as a courtesy toward a lady who merits respect, and out of a sense of occasion. If you don't, she will certainly give no indication that she minds. You have also been warned not to grab or squeeze her hand when it is offered. And you may not initiate conversation; that is her privilege. Wait to be asked something, and do not give lengthy replies if asked a question. Presumably, if possible, 'Yes, Your Majesty' will suffice. It is, after all, more polite not to disagree.

And now a group of people is coming slowly nearer. You cannot see her from the corner of your eye, because she is hidden behind the large man who is making the introductions. You glimpse a woman, but it is someone else – a lady-in-waiting, perhaps. If you cannot see her, you can at least hear her. The quiet murmur of conversation, the interrogative tone as she gently asks a question. There are pauses as she listens. You catch the quick movement, along the line, of ducking heads and hands thrust out. You can hear the rustle of expensive dresses as ladies curtsy. Odd phrases are audible: 'Oh!' 'Really?' 'Is it?' Some distance away, she seems to be genuinely interested in talking to someone. She asks them several things. The exchange lasts a whole minute or so, longer than she is supposed to want to talk to anyone on these occasions. But it comes to an end. 'Well . . .' she says, in a manner that suggests finality, and the little procession continues.

When presentations are made she does not, as Prince Philip or Prince Charles would do, produce some jocular observation that would provoke polite laughter, perhaps making a detail of a person's clothing or accessories the basis for a quip. Nor, like them, would she laugh out loud at something said by others. When they meet the public, they are friendly. When she meets them, she is reserved. She is not here to entertain, so she is quiet and serious, polite but definitely not convivial. The point about what she says is that it is always safe, never opinionated or controversial, even though this may make her seem both uninterested and uninteresting. Did her husband not once say that people would rather be bored than offended? The murmuring increases, you hear her host muttering the name of each person, the questions and responses. 'Had you been there before?' she asks. 'Really?' Although she takes in what is said, she does not react to it, and her tone remains neutral, unemotional, unexcited. She is now on the edge of your vision. You have an impression of a long white dress, and see the shimmer of jewellery. She appears to have a halo but it must be a tiara, glinting with reflected light. She looks pleasantly at those she greets, and her tight smile broadens into a grin when someone mentions a country she has recently visited. When making small talk with strangers, such details can be a godsend. 'What were you doing there?' she asks, matter-of-factly. 'Had you been before? Were you? Yes, beautiful.' Now she is next to you, and then in front of you.

At five foot three she is small, but perhaps not as small as you expected, for in the media she is often pictured standing next to men who tower over her. Recent American presidents, for instance, seem to have been particularly lofty. She is a-dazzle with diamonds. Her hair is very white and her eyes are very blue. Her complexion is legendary for its purity, and this is still true though she is in her eighties. Her posture is as straight as that of her Guardsmen. Her high-heeled shoes are gold and so is her handbag, which is hung from her elbow so that her hand is free. Her smile – a polite baring of the teeth – is hesitant but warm. It is sometimes complained that she does not smile enough but in fact she does so often, especially when listening. She is told your name – there is no reason why she should need to know, yet she frowns slightly as if memorising it – and what your reason is for being present. You look sharply down at your toes, then up again. She offers her hand – a limp touch of gloved fingertips. She holds out only four fingers, not the pinkie. Her voice is low and slightly husky, her speech slow, her diction precise and her accent that of the pre-war upper class. She asks something and you reply: 'Yes, Your Majesty.' Her expression acknowledges this. But your answer was a conversational cul-de-sac. There is nothing further to say. And in any case, you sense your time is up. She knows just how long to spend with each person. She nods and moves on, as do the gaggle of people that surrounds her. She is already talking to someone else: 'Was that the first time you'd been there?' You let out a long breath, thankful you made no mistakes. It does not occur to you, even though you had heard that she finds small talk difficult, that she too might feel relief when such an encounter is over.

Were it not for her jewels and the entourage that follows her, she could have been the benign, retired headmistress of a girls' school. There is about her just that element of what the army calls 'command presence', more than a hint of a brisk and businesslike personality. Nevertheless because her personal reserve is palpable, there was a sense that she was making a particular effort to talk to you, and that is very endearing. You wonder why she has this. After all, she once had Khrushchev to tea, and the Ceausescus to stay. If she could deal with *them*, why would you and your colleagues present a challenge? But it is not the same. With world leaders there are gifts to give and receive and exclaim over, palaces to show them round, important topics to discuss, and there is opportunity to get to know them. Here, there is barely time to exchange greetings with people she will never see again. Yet she does it diligently, sincerely, as if it matters to her.

And then it dawns on you: this is not really shyness anyway. After all, she looked you straight in the eye, and clearly does not lack self-possession. It is a reticence that is carefully calibrated, a well-drilled economy of speech and emotion. There is about her a studied professionalism – after such a long reign you would expect no less – in which dignity, graciousness, interest and friendliness are commodities she measures out and deploys as needed.

Some people would like to see in her public manner more warmth, more humour, more animation. They may even assume, if they know little about her, that the seeming lack of these is due to a cold and formal personality. She is not short of humour, or opinions, but what she cannot afford is to say or do anything controversial. She is well aware how easily any remark or even expression could be misrepresented, misquoted or seen out of context by the media. She will therefore not disagree with anyone, voice strident or even firm views or look in the least disapproving. She is not, in any case, running for office so she does not glad-hand, slap backs, laugh at others' jokes or pretend an interest she does not feel. Politicians do all that, because they must. She does not need to.

She will not, because of the constraints on her time, give you more than minutes or even seconds. What you have just had, in other words, is what everyone gets. She looks earnest and serious, interested, perhaps amused, when performing this task and, for the brief time that she is in conversation, she treats you as the only person in the room. There is none of the self-important person's habit of looking past you, or behaving as if you are not important enough to notice. She is genuinely, if distantly, charming and it is difficult not to be enchanted. You remember reading somewhere how her father told her that anyone who met her would remember the experience for the rest of their life, and you realise that you will.

As soon as she has gone there is an outburst of noise and excitement all around you. 'Thank you all!' bellows whoever was in charge, 'that seemed to go well.' 'So dignified!' people gush. 'Wasn't she charming?' Some are even skittish, light-headed: 'What did she say to you?' they ask each other. No one says, 'Well, that was an ordeal!' because they were all caught up, willingly or otherwise, in the thrill of the moment. Even those who are indifferent to the monarchy can be overcome at meeting the most famous woman of our time, and without exception they found the experience inspiring, intriguing or at the very least deeply interesting. It is a milestone in their lives, deserving of a whole page in the photograph-album of memory. There is, after all, something marvellous about being noticed, acknowledged, spoken to by the Head of State, knowing that with all she has to do and all the important people she has met, she has given you her time and attention, if only for an instant. 'Pinch me, someone!' says a person nearby. Inanity, of course, but that is what a brush with magic is like, and you feel it even if you're a little surprised at yourself for doing so. When you, and the others, get home there will be questions to answer about what she was wearing and what she said, and you will be glad to spread the magic, to sprinkle farther some of the stardust. From now on when anyone asks you: 'Have you ever met the Queen?' you can say yes. If, however, they then enquired: 'What is she like?', how would you answer them? For you still don't know.

# INTRODUCTION

Queen Elizabeth II is, by a considerable margin, the most important woman in the world. By virtue of position, longevity, personality, exposure and influence she has outdistanced and outlasted any other who might have claims on public awareness. Some have undoubtedly held the world's attention, shaped events, demonstrated compassion, led social trends or – briefly – had more 'news value' in terms of the media: Eva Perón, Jacqueline Kennedy, Golda Meir, Indira Gandhi, Margaret Thatcher, Mother Teresa. None has had anything like the position on the world stage occupied by the Queen. Her nearest competitor in the 20th century has been, ironically, her own mother, who died in 2002 at the age of 101. As regards her place in world history Elizabeth II is, without question, going to rank with the great female rulers: Queen Victoria, Catherine the Great, Maria Theresa and the first Elizabeth. Although all of these – even Victoria – wielded greater power than she does, her influence is probably just as great. She is, after all, Head of State in a quarter of the globe and ruler of more independent territories than any sovereign in history.

Careers in public life usually last no more than a decade or two. Politicians are, to a surprising extent, quickly forgotten.

It seems extraordinary – and it is – that when Elizabeth II came to the throne Winston Churchill was Prime Minister, Harry Truman was President of the USA and Russia was ruled by Stalin. She has known – and shared the stage with – a host of other figures who many know only from history books and archive film: Charles de Gaulle, John F. Kennedy, Richard Nixon, Harold Macmillan. For the past 60 years she been privy to every national secret and has worked with every British government and with the leaders of Commonwealth states, as well as travelling to most of the countries in the world. Through her own experience she is linked to many of the great personalities of the later 20th century, and her contact with them has been both formal and light-hearted: when she visited Washington during Eisenhower's presidency she could remind him that a decade earlier, when he was a general and she was a princess, she had taught him to dance an eightsome reel. Through her family she is entwined with even more international events: her husband's mother was honoured by Israel as 'Righteous Among the Nations' for sheltering Jews in Athens during the Holocaust, though it also happens that one of her cousins, the Duke of Coburg, was a Nazi *Gauleiter*. Further back in history, the chain of coincidence is equally intriguing. Her Majesty is not only descended from King George III but from his American antagonist, George Washington.

She is, by nature, quietly dutiful. The British have come to regard this as normal in sovereigns, for George V and VI have also been of this type. While this gives journalists less to write about, it makes the monarchy inoffensive – therefore popular – and provides society with a feeling of stability. Queen Elizabeth is, to a large extent, taken for granted by many of her own subjects. None of them under the age of 60 will have known any other ruler. She has been there all their lives, and appears ageless – at any rate she continues to pursue an active and demanding round of duties. She remains ubiquitous in

British life – broadcasting every Christmas Day, appearing in the news as she opens something or tours a city or welcomes a visiting Head of State. Her face is a national icon, endlessly seen on postcards and plates and tea towels. It is on every stamp her subjects stick and on every coin they spend – and the number of these runs into billions. Occasionally she is criticised in the media for looking glum or for dressing unimaginatively, but if this is true it is not enough to threaten national approval ratings that consistently stay between 80 and 90 per cent. Mostly, coverage of her is respectful, and therefore may seem dull.

It is often a good deal livelier in other countries for, though she herself is usually treated with respect, the stories reported there are frequently exaggerations or outright inventions. Without the constraints of deference or litigation that apply in Britain, journalists can afford to be more colourful. *France Dimanche*, for instance, specialises in reporting alleged quarrels in the Royal Family – it has frequently predicted the Queen's imminent divorce – as well as numerous threats to abdicate. Abroad, the notion of a monarch is, in any case, often something of a novelty. When she went to St Petersburg (the first British monarch to do so) in 1994, a member of the public was quoted as saying: 'We see presidents all the time, but how often do we have a visit from a real queen?' When a German was asked what is the function of his country's Federal President – for the government is run by the Chancellor – he thought for an instant and replied: 'It means we have someone to meet the Queen when she comes on visits.' She is, in other words, a reference point – an affirmation of their own importance – even for people in countries with which she has no connection. More than two centuries after American independence, this descendant of the Colonies' former ruler is sometimes seen as more than a VIP when she goes to the USA. In 2007 she visited Richmond, Virginia shortly after a number of students at a nearby university had been massacred by a gunman. It was arranged that the Queen meet the families of victims and spend time with them in private conversation. It is difficult to imagine any other foreign dignitary – except perhaps the Pope – doing such a thing.

But what exactly is it that she does? She presides over a country that is run by others. She makes Acts of Parliament – and all sorts of other documents – legal by putting her signature on them. She appoints ministers, ambassadors, bishops, judges and military officers. She gives out medals to those people others have deemed worthy of them. She discusses the state of the country every week with the head of the government, and is allowed to suggest or advise solutions to problems, though she herself cannot even vote. She is required to be constantly on show, so that people throughout her realms will know she is aware of them and interested in what they are doing, and this takes a good deal of her time. She has to represent the nation abroad so as to improve relations with other countries, and to represent it at home by speaking to her people at moments of national significance, as well as by opening important buildings or exhibitions or sporting events. She leads the country's mourning on Remembrance Sunday, and every Christmas she has to appear on television to wish her subjects well for the coming year.

She carries out these tasks because she inherited them. She does so without fuss or complaint, and with considerable expertise. Yet whatever the position into which the Queen was born, she could not have fulfilled her destiny so well had she not had a personality suited to the task. Although chosen by accident of fate, she happens to have a passion for it, a genuine sense of vocation. She has her father's modest and conscientious nature, which helps her survive the numbing boredom of official events. She is also a woman of fixed tastes and habits, and these have not altered in any significant way since she succeeded to the throne. She does not like to see change in her routine or her surroundings. Becoming queen at the age of 25, she very quickly grew into the job – assisted by her husband, her mother and her father's advisors – establishing an infrastructure of work and travel and leisure that she has not substantially altered since. She likes being queen, and she knows she is successful at it, so she has no wish to do things differently. She prefers a life that is planned and predictable and this is as well, for without it she could not cope with the heavy workload she continues to carry. She sees it as a job for life rather than, like her counterparts in the Netherlands, a position from which she can retire. Aware of the extent to which she represents national continuity, she wishes to carry on.

This continuity is reflected even in her appearance. She has not, as most women of her age have done, altered her hairstyle for almost half a century. Nor will she, for it has to look just as it does on coins and banknotes. Although the clothes she wore in the 1950s seem dated when seen in pictures, her personal taste coalesced in the following decade and has not changed significantly since. Naturally her wardrobe is stylish and expensive, but it has never followed fashion to any significant degree – there was never any question of adopting the foibles of the 1960s or 1970s – and dresses seen in photographs from 40 years ago look much the same as those she wears today. Never in fashion, she is never out of fashion. She has not developed fads for pastimes, or cuisine, or travel to particular places. Although she could belong at once to the 'jet-set' if she wished to, she does not care for the lifestyle or most of the hobbies. She has no interest in skiing, sailing, playing golf or tennis, though members of her family do all of these. She has no desire to sit at gaming-tables. She is as passionately interested in horses as when she was a small girl, and as addicted to the decidedly unglamorous pleasures of dog-walking and country life that she has enjoyed since childhood. Her personality and tastes, in other words, formed early and have remained consistent ever since, adding to the sense of timelessness about her that many find reassuring. As with her tastes, so with her attitudes. Princess Elizabeth's views and habits merged seam-lessly with those of her parents and grandmother.

To many, what adds to the impression that she lives in some parallel universe is that she does not express views on the important issues of the moment. She is clearly comfortable with the constitutional position that she remain aloof from the political process. The whole point of a constitutional Head of State is that he or she has no ties to any party, is not to blame for government policy and thus stands apart from the crises that embroil politicians and public, representing the long-term view and keeping matters in perspective. In fact, she is intensely aware of political developments and, after a 60-year reign, is a very experienced observer of the national mood. She meets the Prime Minister every week. She invites senior politi-cians to banquets at Buckingham Palace or to 'dine and sleep' at Windsor. She has numerous opportunities to discuss, or to hear about, issues from those most deeply involved in them. She has plenty of opinions, though these are not made known to the public. In private she is lively, shrewd and surprisingly funny; as impatient with pomposity in others as she is with toadying, and skilled in mimicry. She is largely unflappable, given to quiet annoyance but never explosive rage when some-thing goes wrong, and amused by minor mishaps provided no one is hurt or humiliated by them. She has a spontaneous wit that can cause her guests to burst out laughing (she once asked a friend of Prince Charles who had driven to Windsor Castle for lunch, 'Did you find it all right?') We know these things, because we read about them, but we also know the public will never be allowed to see this side of her.

Much is known about her hobbies and pursuits (the Turf, the *Daily Telegraph* crossword, detective novels, enormous jigsaws). Thanks to an insatiable appetite for royal trivia, many people now know that she breakfasts on cereal kept in Tupperware containers. Some of these are half-truths, untruths or speculations anyway. She is said to hate shellfish, since they are banned from menus when she is abroad on state visits. That may not be for reasons of personal preference, but rather because any ill effects from eating them could ruin her timetable and involve letting down people who have waited to see her. Her aversion to avocados, however, is well documented. She thinks they taste 'like soap'.

Much is also known about the important experiences of her past life, simply because it has always been lived in public. Even such a personal matter as meeting and falling for her future husband has been, if we are to believe the account of her former governess, told in detail. Nevertheless she has kept private an enormous amount about herself. Unlike her husband and her children, she does not give interviews – though she has occasionally offered personal memories as part of a documentary. In this reticence she has followed the example of her mother who, despite a sociable and outgoing nature, maintained strict silence with regard to journalists until the very end of her life (when she spoke on television at the time of her 100th birthday, many viewers had never previously heard her voice). Given the media-savvy ways of the Royal Family's younger generations, it is unlikely there will ever again be a monarch who retains such a sense of mystique as Elizabeth II.

She has never gone to school, never done housework or even her own packing, never carried or seriously handled money (the banknote she puts in a church collection is passed to her by an Equerry). All of these things are, of course, a result of her position. Even the circumstances in which she must take her chances with fate, however, have gone without a hitch. Every one of her children and grandchildren has been born healthy. She herself has never known a day's serious illness. Although she fell in love with the first eligible man she encountered, at an age when it might have been argued that she could not have known her own mind, she has been happily married to him for her entire adult life. She has never experienced frustrated love, nor the pain of divorce, though her sister – sadly – knew both.

However rarefied the world in which she moves, the Queen has, to a larger extent than people perhaps realise, participated in the events of the 20th century. Her exalted position does not guard her against the slings and arrows of fortune. Given the long military tradition of her family, her male relatives have seen their share of danger. Her father was at the Battle of Jutland. Her future husband – of whom at that time she was already fond – saw action in the Mediterranean and risked his life on the convoys. Her second son was in the Falklands campaign, and more recently her grandson Prince Harry served for 10 weeks in Afghanistan. One of her mother's brothers was killed in the First World War, and another was a POW. Her uncle, the Duke of Kent, was killed in the Second World War while aboard an RAF aircraft. Even in peacetime there have been tragedies: her cousin, Prince William of Gloucester, also perished in an air crash, in 1972. Her husband's uncle, Lord Mountbatten, was murdered by IRA terrorists in 1979. She and her parents lived through the Blitz, in which their London home – Buckingham Palace – was deliberately targeted by the Luftwaffe and badly damaged.

She and her family are familiar with stress and danger, and her life has contained plenty of anxious, awful moments. Apart from these extreme circumstances, she has known the trauma of her three eldest children's unhappy marriages, and periodic pressure to make household economies, since her finances are often commented upon in the media. She has even, despite the presence of policemen, Household regiments and all manner of ceremonial bodyguards to protect her, awoken to find a prowler in her bedroom. Although the scale of her surroundings may be beyond comparison with that of most of her subjects, she too has been subject to adversity.

In spite of the affection with which the public regards her, she has not been able to enjoy the luxury of complacency. IRA terrorism posed a considerable threat to the Royal Family from the early 1970s onward. Even before that she had faced the possibility of violent unrest, from Welsh nationalists at the time of her son's investiture as Prince of Wales (their bombing campaign, minuscule in comparison with what came later, is largely forgotten today), or from Quebec separatists who booed her – and might have done much worse – when she visited Canada in the 1960s. 'Danger,' she once said, 'is part of the job,' and she refuses to let the prospect of assassination interrupt her routine. No matter what layers of security exist between the Queen and the public, she has to have more personal, physical courage than many people realise or appreciate – as was seen in 1981, when a young man fired shots at her as she rode along the Mall.

Her position requires her to be on show, to move among crowds, and therefore to be vulnerable to the shouted insults of drunks or to the assassin's bullet, but she has long since weighed up the risks and decided that she will carry on regardless. On occasion an entire visit has been advised against by the Foreign Office because the host country was deemed too unstable to protect her. This was the case with Ghana in 1958 as guest of the unpopular Kwame Nkrumah. Sitting next to him in a dozen places, she could be injured by some attempt on him. The Queen, overruling her advisors, insisted on going. 'How silly I should look,' she told them, 'if I was scared to visit and then Khrushchev went and had a good reception.' She returned safely, and the tour was a great success. The fact that she has always been sanguine in the face of potential danger is, perhaps, not the least impressive of her qualities.

There are different kinds of courage, and she must have several of them. The Queen lives on a constant and unrelenting diet of bad tidings. She watches the news like the rest of us, but she often knows more than we do. During the Cold War she will have had far greater knowledge of the dangers to peace – and the risk of nuclear annihilation – than her people. Imagine the stress her position must have involved during the crises over Berlin and Cuba. Yet through it all she maintained an apparently genuine sense of calm, and carried on with her job, including the archaic ceremonial, as if nothing were amiss. Murders, terrorist outrages, natural disasters at home or in the Commonwealth and beyond – all these are reported to her because there is often something official she is required to do, such as sending condolences or expressing the nation's sorrow. As already seen, when visiting an American city she met the families of those killed by a frenzied gunman. Whatever can you say to console *one* person in those circumstances, let alone a whole series of grieving relatives? It cannot have been easy, and they were not even her subjects, yet she did it.

Suppose that, like her grandfather George V in the years between the wars, she feels that society is going to the dogs. This is distinctly possible, given that she is an elderly lady of traditional bent who has very high personal standards of morals and integrity. She not only cannot publicly disapprove of things, she may be obliged to sign the very legislation that legalises what was previously unacceptable. This takes courage too. As one of her Private Secretaries, Sir John Colville, put it: 'By sheer strength of willpower the Queen controls the impatience she must often feel, and never fails to look imperturbable. Nothing is better calculated to win the esteem of her subjects.' Besides courage, she has several advantages that have helped to make her the effective ruler she is. The first was training, the second was temperament, the third was routine and the fourth was advice.

From the age of 10 – when her uncle abdicated – she was intensively schooled for the position she would occupy. She worked very closely with her father, whose style and tastes she consciously continued, and in the early part of her own reign used many of the same advisors and officials. She and her father had had, in fact, the same tutor – Queen Mary (1867–1953), redoubtable widow of King George V, who trained them rigorously in the correct performance of duty. Once described as 'the most queenly of queens', Mary's rigid bearing can be

seen at a glance in old photographs. She was expert in protocol and appropriate behaviour, instilling an indelible sense of
service by which personal wishes, and feelings, were entirely
secondary to the demands of duty, just as she educated her
granddaughter to appreciate the cultural riches that make up
the Royal Collections. It is worth remembering that this influence was directed at Elizabeth for the first 25 years of her life,
and will have taken on added importance when she became
heir – a thorough and intensive indoctrination of a willing
pupil who responded by modelling herself on the old lady.
If a certain toughness of character has been passed on, that
is hardly surprising. What she also inherited, however, was a
lifelong awareness of the need to justify her position by hard
work and goodwill.

Elizabeth was also, and more specifically, taught by her
father. Having had no preparation for his own succession,
he wanted to ensure that she was fully ready for hers. Queen
Victoria would not let her eldest son see the contents of
dispatch boxes; George VI habitually sent for his daughter to
go through his with him. The first time she took the salute
at Trooping the Colour he gave her a rigorous inspection of
uniform and drill before she left the Palace. From her mother's example she learned how to charm – how to talk easily to
others – even though her own personality did not enable her
to do this so effectively. Everywhere around her were mentors,
teachers, examples. She grasped the importance of what she
was doing, and strove to do it well. The Queen's formative
years were, of course, interrupted by the Second World War.
Because she did not attend school or university, it might be
assumed that she lacks the intellectual discipline to analyse and
retain information. In fact, she was soundly, privately educated
in the subjects – history and constitutional law, for instance
– that had bearing on her future. She may not have had the
stimulus of a school environment, or the spur of examinations
or of competition with other pupils, but she had the benefit

of one-to-one tuition and her intellectual training, if limited in scope, was excellent. Because she came to the throne when young, she has also had the experience of learning her job by doing it.

Her second advantage was temperament. It is a point worth emphasising that Elizabeth never had what might be called a 'Prince Hal phase', in which she rebelled against her upbringing or her destiny. She accepted it and prepared for it and looked forward to it. Her views never clashed with those of her family or the people who sought to train her. While her uncle David, as King Edward VIII, often ignored the red dispatch boxes sent to him by the government, Queen Elizabeth makes a point of reading everything in hers, going through them for an hour or two each evening. Through concentration and long practice she can absorb and retain large amounts of information and weigh its implications. The Queen has an extremely good memory for both facts and faces. On subjects that engage her interest, such as art and antiques, she has amassed considerable knowledge. On the breeding, training and racing of horses, her lifelong enthusiasm, she has a level of expertise that is overwhelming.

Although these are leisure interests, her grasp of social and political matters is just as detailed. The politician Tony Benn, no admirer of monarchy, said of her: 'She is not very clever but is remarkably intelligent.' She is not clever in the sense of being widely read, but is extremely well-versed in matters that relate to her role. With her powerful memory, she can also quickly 'mug up' on a matter in order to discuss it. And there are subjects she has studied in detail over long years. For someone who cannot vote, for example, she has an intense knowledge of the British electoral system, the state of the parties, and the personalities in the Commons. She studies all the documents she is given by advisors, and retains a surprising amount of what she reads. She can grasp essentials, reel off statistics, recall past conversations. This is a matter of memory. Although there is an agenda for discussion during her weekly meetings with the Premier, no one has seen the Queen taking notes, and by custom no written record is ever kept of these. She need not pay such close attention, for after all she cannot alter anything that Parliament has decided, but she considers all this information useful. She has an instinct borne of long practice for knowing how the British people will react to things – reading their mood, taking the temperature – and she can use this to give advice.

Dealing, over decades, with the leaders of other countries and the prime ministers of her own has given her a wealth of experience that aids her judgement. Not only that, but she has personal associations with a huge array of world statesmen, and can counsel politicians to whom these people are only names. It is a long-established cliché that she can catch out government ministers by knowing more than they do about a specific subject, or embarrass them with questions they cannot answer. This is something of a game. She has been quietly scoring points in the same way ever since her audiences were with Winston Churchill, and her father did it too. It is somewhat unfair, for she is now vastly more experienced than any of her politicians and has discussed similar, or the same, issues with their predecessors-in-office, literally for generations. It must also be borne in mind that she has far greater opportunities to see the wider picture than her ministers do. 'She has sources of information that no one else has,' as one observer put it. Much that goes on in Whitehall is seen on a 'need to know' basis, but the Queen can see everything. Even without her special access, she learns much simply by doing her homework. She is always, in a phrase used about barristers, 'on top of her brief', and this is not easy considering the fact that all areas of national and commonwealth life come within the scope of her job.

From formal meetings and stilted small talk she can extract a surprising amount of useful knowledge. President Bill Clinton noticed this, recalling that: 'I was taken with the clever manner in which she discussed public issues, probing me for information without venturing too far into expressing her own political views.' He added: 'She impressed me as someone who might have become a successful politician or diplomat. As it was she had to be both, without seeming to be either.' This is a very eloquent summing-up of her role.

At conferences of Commonwealth heads of government she will have a private audience with each of them. In the space of a few minutes she can discuss the issues facing Australia, both listening and advising, and then go on to do the same for Tuvalu or Mozambique. Her dispatch boxes, after all, contain papers relating not only to the governance of Britain. They also include reams of confidential information about the countries of the Commonwealth. From the Dominions, she also receives reports from the Governors-General that even the prime ministers do not see. And she is extremely observant. Schooled by a long lifetime of protocol and formality, she knows exactly how things should be done and will quickly notice any mistakes, whether it be a diplomat wearing an order incorrectly, cutlery laid in the wrong manner at a banquet, or a soldier fumbling a drill-movement. Moreover she will notice, and remember, individual faces in a crowd – on the first tour of Canada after her accession she recognised, from her previous visit three years earlier, one of the mounties guarding her, and greeted him warmly. Although she can be critical when she feels dignity has been undermined, she is usually sympathetic – and even heartily amused – if some much-rehearsed event goes awry, for it adds excitement to duties that are otherwise predictable. When igniting the first of the chain of bonfires on a rainy evening at Windsor to celebrate her Silver Jubilee, the torch failed to stay alight and then the beacon erupted into flame before she could reach it. 'Oh good, what fun!' was her comment.

Whenever she is the hostess at an event, she will make a point of inspecting the arrangements, probably several times, in advance. Before guests arrive at Windsor she will go through their rooms, checking that everything they need is correctly laid out. When she is to meet people even superficially, such as during one of the 13 investiture ceremonies held each year, she will read notes about them in advance so that she knows what to expect, and has some conversational starting point – even though there will be a 150 of them. Many countries' governments employ a chief of protocol for the organising of official events. In Britain the Head of State herself knows all that is necessary.

The third element is routine. The Queen has repeatedly carried out all the functions of state: opening Parliament, hosting – or making – official visits, so often that she knows every detail about what happens, when and how. When she celebrates her official birthday in June with the military parade called Trooping the Colour – to cite but one example – it is worth remembering that not only has she presided at this dozens of times (it has only once in her reign been cancelled, owing to a rail strike), but that she will also, each year, have met the principal people involved, listened to and approved all the music that will be played, and received reports on how rehearsals for the event are going. She is not only Commander in Chief of the Armed Forces and Colonel-in-Chief of the Household Division, she is also known to be an expert on army uniforms and to have an extremely practised eye for the details of drill, so she knows precisely how the complex manoeuvring of men and mounts should be carried out. Of the regiments taking part, her husband, her eldest son, her daughter and her cousin and one of her grandsons are colonels of five, while two of her grandsons are serving officers in one. No change in dress or movement, no matter how trivial, could be made without her approval. As she watches the troops she will know the names of many officers and NCOs, and even of some of the horses. But then she has participated in more of these occasions than anyone else present, including her husband. Although today she travels to the parade ground by carriage she was meticulous, in the years when she attended on horseback, in practising for it just as her soldiers did.

The fourth element is advice. The Queen is exhaustively briefed on the places she goes and the people she meets. She has expert counsel whenever she needs it (the Foreign Secretary, for instance, may accompany her on a state visit), and she studies the reports or other materials submitted to her. If she visits a British city she will have on hand the Lord Lieutenant, the mayor and, probably, the entire local council executive to tell her about it. In all the types of situation mentioned above, she receives as well as dispenses wisdom. No matter where she is, she has access to a constant flow of documents and press digests that ensure she is supremely well informed. Her Private Secretaries have, without exception, been men of high calibre and ability, and they are with her everywhere, smoothing the way. Nothing is ever left to chance, nothing is ever improvised at the last moment, and it shows.

The Queen is very happy with such arrangements. She could not possibly meet the demands on her time if a great many people were not constantly helping her. Everything she needs must be immediately at her elbow, whether this means a breakfast tray in the morning, a car at the door, or – until relatively recently – the Royal Yacht moored opposite some foreign port when she arrived for a state visit. She has an extensive, well-trained and efficient staff to manage all the complexities of her very active life. Her lady-in-waiting not only has to ensure that spare gloves and shoes, barley sugar and handkerchiefs are to hand, she must also ascertain in advance of an official visit where the 'facilities' are, since it would be unthinkable for Her Majesty to have to ask her hosts. The Queen appreciates such effort, knows the names of even her minor servants and rewards them with presents every Christmas. Like all members of the Royal Family, she values the loyalty of those who work for her and does not like the faces around her to change.

As the royal biographers Graham and Heather Fisher have said: 'The Queen's life has almost the same built-in monotony as a car-worker on a production-line, and some people would find it just as boring.' This is perhaps a poor comparison, since Her Majesty has a constant change of scenery and a great deal of what she sees is colourful, impressive, informative and amusing. Nevertheless boredom is certainly likely. It is a commonplace that many of her subjects would wish to take her place ... for a day, to see what being Queen is like. The thought of weeks, let alone months or years, of an often stultifying routine would be deeply off-putting to anyone with creativity, independence, imagination or an impatience with social pleasantries. The thing about it that they might find most onerous is the absence of any complete holiday or the prospect of never retiring. And the Queen's is not a life that allows for spontaneity. There can be no question of taking in a film on impulse, going shopping to cheer herself up or dropping in unannounced on old friends. And there is no question of being pleasantly surprised to find what is for lunch since every meal she has will have been chosen, probably days in advance, from a menu (in French). Even the books read by the Royal Family are selected for them each year by a committee, which strikes a balance between light and serious subject matter and forwards the chosen titles to the Palace. Everything the Queen does is planned to the smallest detail, usually months ahead. But then this has been true since, as a girl of 10, she became heir to the throne. It is what she knows and expects and is comfortable with. As for boredom, she has acknowledged that 'some occasions are less interesting than others', but usually there is diversion to be found somewhere if one keeps a sharp eye out and an open mind.

It is also a life that allows for very few friendships. The Queen has some, of course – women she knew as a child, racing enthusiasts and old families whose members have been friends of the Royals for generations. It is simply not possible, however, to have more than a very small circle of trusted inti-mates. For the rest, the Queen is gracious but distant. As one of her prime ministers, James Callaghan, put it: 'What one gets from the Queen is friendliness, but not friendship.'

Elizabeth II is by far the most widely travelled monarch in British – and indeed in world – history. In many places she goes, to be a monarch is unusual, and carries distinction. To be Europe's longest-serving, high-profile example of the breed brings even greater prestige. There are few people in any region of the world that can be reached by television or the printed word who have not at least seen a picture of the Queen. She is thus already familiar to most of those who line processional routes to watch her pass. At home her subjects, shivering through a British winter, may feel a pang of envy at the sight of her on a Pacific island, but they would probably not relish the crowded and unforgiving official schedule she has to follow. It is difficult to appreciate what a chore these overseas visits must be. When, in 1976, she visited Bloomingdale's store in New York, she had less than 15 minutes to look around. When in the National Gallery in Washington, she had no more than 20 minutes to take in the wealth of pictures. Although she was accompanied by the gallery's director, who would have shown her the highlights, she would be unlikely to take away more than a blurred impression of them. She has, because of her own collection, considerable interest in paintings, and would undoubtedly have wanted to spend a longer time there.

These occasions are not, of course, holidays, and there are no grounds for envying her the chance to see so many parts of the world. Although her timetable may well include a day or more set aside for rest and privacy on some remote country estate, she seldom has opportunities for the pleasures others take for granted when abroad: leisurely browsing in local markets, dawdling in museums, spending mornings at a café table writing postcards. Most women, when on a trip overseas, would not want to have to dress all the time in a hat and gloves and coat. The Queen is, of course, required to dress formally, meet endless people on a superficial basis, make speeches, and catch only tantalising glimpses of things that cannot – owing to the pressures of time and protocol – be enjoyed in detail. She sees not what she would like to but what her hosts want her to. When she is abroad and travelling by car or train, she often cannot even enjoy the passing scenery, for she will be having to work at her dispatch boxes, prepare herself for a speech she will be giving at the next stop, or read through reams of briefing notes about people and places she will be encountering in the hours, or days, ahead. It is worth remembering that most of the work she does is out of sight and behind the scenes. As with an accomplished actress the public see only the finished performance, not the rehearsals, the costume-fittings or the lengthy production meetings.

Like many people for whom routine travel on business has made holidays abroad less interesting, the Queen prefers to spend her leisure time in homely and familiar surroundings – weekends at Windsor, Christmas at Sandringham, summers cruising off the Highlands, autumns at Balmoral. Being fair-skinned she does not like strong sun, and thus has no desire to spend her leisure time on a Mediterranean beach. Understandably what she relishes most is privacy and the space to indulge in her favourite outdoor activities. She has great affection for familiar scenes, and the Scottish landscape in particular offers a lifetime of pleasant memory. Some people might wonder that she prefers the damp and midges of Scotland, but she has said that her ideal relaxation is 'a couple of weeks in the rain at Balmoral'. She makes only occasional unofficial – and very little known – private forays abroad, in pursuit of equine interests, to France or Kentucky. Although with five homes she can always have a change of scene, it is worth remembering that she is never free from the duties of her position. She receives red dispatch boxes from the Government each day, filled with documents that must be read and often signed. She works on these no matter where she is.

At every stage of her life she has been described in a flood of words. There are numerous biographies of her in print, and jumble sales yield an invariable harvest of pictorial souvenir albums that commemorate the milestones in her life: marriage, coronation, children, jubilees, wedding anniversaries and state visits.

And these are only the books. Since the advent of the modern media and its more active Royal Correspondents there has been an unceasing tide of copy devoted to her. Some of this has been intrusive, some critical, but most has been respectful, obsequious, even cloying. Penelope Mortimer, when researching a biography of the Queen Mother, memorably described the experience of reading about her as 'like swimming through treacle'. The respectful tone of much that is written rightly puts off some of the reading public, yet it is hardly the Queen's fault that she is described in such terms. It is a matter of fact, rather than fawning hyperbole, that she fulfils her role extremely well, as did her mother.

The Queen is acutely aware of her place in history. She is the seventh English monarch to be queen in her own right, and she has had important 'role models' in the shape of her two great predecessors, Elizabeth I and Victoria. She is proud of following them on the throne. She is proud of the things her era has added to the national experience and of the bridges, hospitals, universities and other monuments – some of them bearing her name – that will last for centuries as a memorial to her reign.

One strand of opinion has it that the monarchy somehow holds back the progress of Britain – that this feudal way of doing things is an insult to an intelligent people and that it means the country is known for archaic flummery rather than innovation in science and the arts. An intelligent observer would find little evidence of this – the Rolls-Royce engine is known throughout the world regardless of who is Head of State – but would discover a great deal of proof that the country is respected abroad because of the Queen. The age of Elizabeth II is likely to be compared with that of Elizabeth I in one important respect – the flowering of culture. This has gone on unhindered by of the presence of monarchy, and often with its support. There is no likelihood that the era over which Queen Elizabeth has presided will in retrospect be seen as reactionary or backward-looking as was, say, the rule of Franco in Spain. Her realm is not, in any important sense, a museum. It has given the world The Beatles, and punk rock, and the theatre of John Osborne. It produces world-class engineers, architects, authors, fashion designers, rock musicians. Her subjects win Oscars and Nobel Prizes and Olympic medals, unhampered by the supposed obsolescence of their country's constitutional arrangements. Indeed for a large proportion of these people, meeting the Queen and receiving from her some accolade is just as great a personal triumph.

It is difficult to write of Queen Elizabeth II in terms other than warm admiration, for she does not merit any other treatment. There are no critical biographies of the Queen, and it is unlikely there will be. She simply provides no target for criticism. She has never abused her position, her privileges or her influence. She has never stood in the way of change. She has never put her own comfort, wishes or interests above her duty. She has never become involved in controversy, financial irregularity or political favouritism. The only time her subjects have been able to find fault with her – and that only for a matter of days – was when she gave no public sign of grief after the death of Princess Diana. It was a strange period in which the attacks on the Queen hurt and baffled her, for she has never had to become used to grumbling from the inhabitants of middle Britain, and it is very difficult to imagine that such an experience will occur again. Otherwise, her public and private lives have been blameless. If this makes her dull, the world could do with a lot more dullness.

If you look clearly at what the Queen does and how she does it, I defy you not to be impressed. You might subscribe to the disparagement of monarchy that is fashionable in some circles. You might have no interest in historic ceremony, nor see in it any worthwhile purpose. You might – if you have no views on racing or horse-breeding or the countryside – dread the thought of talking to her. But you will respect her. Because she deserves it.

# PRINCESS, 1926–1939

'Isn't it lucky that Lilibet's the eldest?'

Running westward from Bond Street to Berkeley Square, Bruton Street is in the midst of London's Mayfair. Today it is largely associated with the galleries of clothing designers, whose names appear on their shopfronts. The buildings are unremarkable; the older ones consisting of five-storey dwellings whose ground floors have been, without exception, converted to commercial purposes. Not a single private house remains. These are not grand dwellings by the standards of Grosvenor Square or Belgravia. There is no parade of stuccoed pillars such as one would find in Eaton Square, nor the towering brick gables of Cadogan Place. There is a modest intimacy here.

Number 17 is now a very modern office block. Eighty years ago, on this site, was the town house of the Earl of Strathmore. He was the maternal grandfather of Princess Elizabeth, and it was here that she was born. No plaque marks the spot, and the only visible link with royalty is that directly opposite are the former premises – this time there *is* a plaque – of Norman Hartnell, who was to design many of her clothes. Here were created the dresses she wore for both her wedding and her Coronation.

But this is to anticipate. Princess Elizabeth came into the world by Caesarean section on 21 April 1926, at 2:40 a.m. Her father was Albert ('Bertie') Duke of York, second son of King George V and brother of David, the Prince of Wales. Her mother was the former Elizabeth Bowes-Lyon, a member of an illustrious Scottish noble family. The Princess's father did not possess the glamour of his brother, the Prince of Wales. He had little confidence, spoke with a stammer and would fly into frustrated rages. He was also kind and thoroughly decent, devoted to his family and dutiful to a fault. If he lacked his brother's charisma he also lacked his self-centred hedonism. Lady Elizabeth Bowes-Lyon was born in 1900, growing up during the Great War and 'coming out' into the vacuous gaiety of the 1920s. As a debutante she was immensely popular. She was extremely good company, her gifts of conversation and humour honed by years of ministering to wounded soldiers at her parents' home, and several young men were in love with her. Despite belonging to the 'jazz age', she had about her none of the frivolous, cocktails-and-laughter characteristics that caused the King to disapprove so completely of young women of the time. She won his entire approval – no mean feat, for his standards were exacting – and he advised his son that: 'You'll be a lucky fellow if she accepts you.' Bertie, in fact, asked her twice before she did. It was not the Duke himself who made her hesitate, but the thought of marrying into his family. She was not, of course, to realise that the path she chose would take her to the throne and make her one of the most popular queens in history. Her mother had said of him that: 'He is a man who will be made or marred by marriage.' This proved to be true, and he was most fortunate in his choice.

Princess Elizabeth was not heir to the throne – it was still thought likely at the time that her 32-year-old uncle would marry and produce his own offspring – but she was the first grandchild within the immediate Royal Family. Her presence also meant that there were three generations of Royals and this promise for the future, as it always does, provided the British public with a reassuring sense of continuity. She represented good news to a country in turmoil, for the General Strike began a week after her birth. While there was no reason to assume that the little girl would become queen, this possibility was not ignored. As one author, Dermot Morrah, has said: 'The idea that Princess Elizabeth would one day become Queen Elizabeth II was never altogether remote from the thoughts of her future subjects. Imperceptibly as the years went by it changed from a conscious speculation to a possibility and then to a probability.' It was also quite likely that, even if she did not inherit the British throne, she might become the queen of some other country through marriage. From the very beginning of her life she was therefore the subject of widespread public curiosity, speculation and affection. This would increase as she grew into an attractive and photogenic infant with curly fair hair, who smiled readily. It would be consolidated when she was joined, a few years later, by an equally attractive sister.

She might have spent her infant years in Canada, for there was some notion in the mid-1920s of her father being appointed Governor-General there. The King, however, felt that this would be too great a trial for his diffident son, and the idea was not pursued.

The Princess's father may have been disappointed at not having had a boy. If so, he never gave any sign of it. On the contrary he was a model parent who, like his wife, was absolutely devoted to his daughters, and the Duchess had, in any case, wanted a girl. For a few years it remained a possibility that the birth of a brother would oust Elizabeth from her place in the succession, but when, in 1930, a second daughter, Margaret, was also born by Caesarean section, the matter ended. In those days it was considered dangerous to have more than two such operations, and the Duchess was warned by her doctors that there could be no more children. It was at that time that Elizabeth's grandmother began to see her as a likely heir and to train her for a future on the throne.

The Princess was christened, five weeks after birth, by the Archbishop of Canterbury in the chapel at Buckingham Palace, wrapped in the same Honiton lace garment as had been used for her father, grandfather and great-grandfather. The names chosen for her – Elizabeth Alexandra Mary – referred to her mother, grandmother and great-grandmother (who had just died), although curiously these were not in sequence, with Alexandra coming in the middle and not last.

Very early in her life – she was not yet two – the Princess was left in the care of servants and grandparents while the Duke and Duchess went on an official tour to Australia. They missed her first birthday as a result ('We are not supposed to be human,' lamented her mother). Her time was divided between her Strathmore relations, at their Scottish and English homes, and the King and Queen. Neither King George nor Queen Mary had a natural flair for children. Both had been distant, formal and demanding parents. The King, notorious for his rages, had terrified his sons and grandsons, but took at once to this little girl, whom he spoiled. She was to visit him during his recovery from illness at Bognor, for she was unfailingly able to cheer him up. He liked to have breakfast with Elizabeth and, when at Sandringham, to take her on visits to his stud. She was thus aware from infancy of the atmosphere of stables and of their silent, dignified occupants. The seeds of a lifetime's passion were sown here.

When her parents returned from overseas the little Princess appeared with them on the Palace balcony as they acknowledged the cheers of the crowd. It was her first public appearance. She was so much the centre of attention that the Duke and Duchess had been presented on their travels with no less than three tons of toys for her. She received a few of them, but the great majority were given to children in hospital.

Although she was always a Royal Highness, Elizabeth herself invented the name by which she has been known to intimates ever since. 'Lilibet' was her early attempt to enunciate her own name, and somehow it stuck. More than 80 years later, she still uses it when signing Christmas cards to relatives and old friends.

At the age of three, she was featured on the cover of *Time* magazine – then, as now, a considerable accolade. She was dressed in yellow, and this started a trend throughout the world for children's clothing in that colour. This was not all. She was also depicted on a stamp (six cents, Newfoundland) and appeared on several commercial products. A section of the Antarctic was even named in her honour. When she was four, the first biography of her was published – *The Story of Princess Elizabeth* by Anne Ring.

There was to be more in a similar vein throughout the years ahead – words and pictures that showed a happy family, with two bright and attractive daughters, surrounded by pets in agreeable garden settings. The Duchess, who allowed these intrusions, has been accused of 'marketing' her family by arranging access for photographers and writers, manipulating what would now be called 'the media' in order to present them as middle-class paragons.

What was the point of such a public-relations exercise? The age into which the girls were born was not one of established order and social certainties but a time of extremes, both economic and political. The Great War had recently toppled the thrones of their family's continental relatives, and no monarchy could afford complacency. The public's loyalty could no longer be taken for granted. It must be earned – and kept – by constant effort. In Britain, industrial relations were bad, unemployment was widespread and envy of the rich was consequently rife. The House of Windsor must be seen to justify the goodwill and respect that its members still commanded. To live modestly and unostentatiously as the Yorks, by royal standards, did was in keeping with the spirit of the age, and increased the popularity of the monarchy. To feature in the press as a charming, pleasant and ordinary family, devoted to useful work and high domestic ideals, was to provide escapism for those whose lives were grimmer.

The image that the Duchess enabled the public to see was in no sense a sham. She and her family really were as wholesome, unpretentious and devoted to each other as the images suggested. The family provided a welcome boost to national morale throughout the years of the Depression. By the time she came to the throne, Elizabeth's popularity had been building for a quarter of a century.

Her sister, Margaret, was four years her junior. They grew up to be extremely close, for their position made it difficult to befriend others, and they did not go to school. The girls looked very similar. Both had the same chin-length chestnut hair and blue eyes. The resemblance was increased by the things they wore: they were always dressed, if not the same, then at least similarly. Their clothes were plain and practical and, even for the time, often quaintly old-fashioned: dresses cut identically – although sometimes in different colours – sensible brown shoes and calf-length white socks. The only differences, and these were trivial, were that Elizabeth had her hair parted on the right and Margaret on the left, and that the older sister wore three strings of pearls while the younger had only two. She became resentful, however, if her sister had something she did not: 'Margaret always wants what I have,' Elizabeth complained. This was never more obvious than at their father's Coronation. The elder daughter, as heir, was given a gown with a train and a scaled-down coronet. Margaret made sufficient fuss to be given these too, although she had to make do with a shorter train.

Their closeness was in spite of having very different personalities. Elizabeth was earnest, conscientious, eager to please and to do what was expected of her. Margaret was comical, wilful, irreverent and mischievous, a gifted singer and mimic who loved performing and had a talent for wheedling her way out of tasks she disliked. Elizabeth had a temper inherited from her father and grandfather, but this was not often seen. She disliked confrontation, in fact, and would let her sister have her way to avoid it. Margaret was very aware of being the second child and thus of receiving less interest and less privilege, but for the same reason she was given more leeway by her parents and was more spoiled. The girls themselves were aware of the differences in temperament between them. Margaret, comfortable in the role of scamp and rebel, said to her mother: 'Isn't it lucky that Lilibet's the eldest?'

Elizabeth was obsessively tidy, saving – and neatly folding – the wrapping paper from presents. There would never be a time in her life when she would be guilty of sloppiness, either of mind or habit. Although in theory she had always had others to pick up after her, in practice she was never to need much running after.

Yet she was a good deal more energetic, fun-loving and noisy than accounts of her childhood suggest. She was filled with curiosity, wanting to know about the things around her, asking questions of those she encountered and unafraid to talk to strangers because everyone she met treated her with respect. Like her sister, she could amuse grown-ups – as when she was once asked at Sandringham by the Archbishop of Canterbury if she would walk with him in the garden. She agreed, but with the stipulation: 'Please do not tell me anything more about God. I know all about Him already.' Such occasional off-handedness once caused her grandmother to introduce her as 'Princess Elizabeth, who hopes one day to be a lady.'

Her father had seen to it that, from the time she was first conscious of her surroundings, Elizabeth learned to obey her elders and to live up to their expectations, and to do so willingly, just as he had been advised by his own father to learn quickly the habits of obedience and conformity as a means of avoiding trouble. She inherited his personality – painstaking, methodical and dutiful – rather than the warm spontaneity that characterised her mother, but her own inclinations must have concurred with his advice. Years later, a former soldier recalled: 'I was in the Household Cavalry; they have to salute any member of the Royal Family. Princess Elizabeth used to walk by and not take any notice, whereas Princess Margaret would sort of wave.' This should not be seen as evidence of a certain *hauteur*. Rather, it suggests the seriousness with which she took her role. Elizabeth loved the trappings of ceremony that surrounded her family – she was quite capable of walking past the sentries just to see them present arms – and she was interested in those who performed these rituals. She would have been aware, however – even at an early age – that it was both wrong and undignified to distract them while they were going about their duty.

The family had two homes. In London they lived at 145 Piccadilly, a five-storey mansion on the north side whose windows looked across Hyde Park Corner at St George's Hospital and at the gardens of Buckingham Palace. A victim of wartime bombing, its remains were to be cleared away for the widening of Park Lane.

The house would be considered grand enough by most people, although Marion Crawford, the Princesses' governess, described it somewhat extraordinarily as: 'Neither large nor splendid. It might have been the home of any moderately well-to-do young couple starting married life.' It happened to have 25 bedrooms, and half-a-dozen staff. The girls lived on the top floor, where a large glass dome shed light on the stairwell. Beneath this, on the landing, they kept an extensive and neatly ordered collection of toy horses, all of which were groomed and exercised.

The residence was situated on the crest of the low hill where Piccadilly sweeps westward up to Hyde Park Corner. To its right was Park Lane and the ornate entrance to the park as well as Apsley House, former home of the Iron Duke. Across from it was the huge memorial arch that commemorated his military career. A reminder of a more recent conflict – the Artillery Memorial – was also nearby. Opposite, behind a low wall and hidden by trees, were the gardens of Buckingham Palace. From their top-floor vantage point the Princesses could see not only noble architecture but the everyday life of London from which, by protocol and a protective barrier of servants, they were excluded. They watched the unending procession of pedestrians and vehicles that passed below. They had a particular fascination with the open-top double-decker buses, and longed to travel in one. They were to do so, but only once, for an IRA bombing campaign led to heightened security measures and ended such outings. They noticed the horses among the traffic, and developed a particular affection for a pair that passed at the same hour each evening, pulling a brewer's dray. They were greatly disappointed if they missed them.

At the back of 145 was a now-vanished green space called Hamilton Gardens. Enclosed by railings and filled with sooty shrubbery, it was linked, by a gate, with Hyde Park. It was the principal playground of the girls and their friends, who were largely cousins or the daughters of neighbours. From the park beyond this small enclosure the Princesses were watched at play by members of the public. Elizabeth and Margaret took for granted the presence of inquisitive spectators. They even reciprocated their curiosity. They were intrigued by the children they saw on their walks in the park, and might smile shyly at them. They were, like closeted royal children everywhere, to develop a fascination with those beyond their own world.

The other, weekend, home of the Yorks was White Lodge in Richmond Park. Both husband and wife disliked it intensely.

It was very inconvenient, stuck in the midst of great swathes of parkland that were entirely accessible to the public, so that there was no privacy. Only in 1932 did they escape to a more secluded house – Royal Lodge at Windsor. This had begun as a shooting-box for George IV, and is a pleasantly rambling Regency building, but at that time it was much in need of repair. Plans had been made for extensive remodelling but, with the onset of the Depression in 1929, had had to be shelved. In response to the country's economic woes, the King cut his own Civil List by half, and his sons had to reduce their expenditure accordingly. Royal Lodge therefore remained rather uncomfortable. Nevertheless it was made habitable and decorated in the Duchess's favoured colours of fawn and pink. It had around it the seemingly limitless expanses of Windsor Great Park with its opportunities for walking and riding. It also had its own enclosed garden, long-since grown into a jungle. The taming of the garden became a passion for the Yorks, who devoted hours at weekends, in old tweeds and sweaters, to clearing and planting. The Princesses became involved in this, and would have known discomfort and blisters – and the fun of getting dirty in a good cause – just as the adults did.

One thing the Yorks did not want to do was to travel abroad. The parents of many aristocratic children of that age would have gone to the Riviera and St Moritz as a matter of course. Elizabeth's parents took their pleasures in Scotland, at Glamis and Balmoral. No doubt the King liked to have them on holiday with him in the Highlands, and his own views on foreign countries ('Abroad is bloody') were well known. Elizabeth might have grown up familiar with other lands, playing with cousins from other Royal Houses (more or less as her future husband was doing). Instead, she was to see nothing of the world until she went to South Africa at the age of 20.

Within a short distance of Royal Lodge was built the Wendy house of every small girl's dreams. 'Y Bwthyn Bach' ('the little house' in Welsh) was a gift from the people of the Principality on her sixth birthday. There was about it nothing of the stage-set, and there was no need for its occupants to make believe, for everything was in working order. The roof of this two-storey building was thatched (it still has to be renewed period-ically), and the rooms (which are too small for adults to stand up in) were fully equipped with working lights, running water and miniature versions of household products and implements – from a dustpan to a vacuum cleaner and a radio – for its maintenance. The girls, needless to say, loved it, not only for its scale and detail but also because it represented an 'ordinary' home. Elizabeth could be as fastidious in her sweeping and cleaning as her tidy nature desired.

As regards other toys, there were constant gifts. Those from members of the public could not, according to protocol, be accepted and so were returned. Those from other sources – organisations, communities and other nations – were kept. Elizabeth had both a baker's van and a grocer's cart, with which she could make deliveries using her governess as the horse. A number of the dolls owned by the Princesses can still be seen at Windsor. They include two Japanese ladies in kimonos and two dolls given to the girls by the President of France. 'France' and 'Marianne' came with beautifully designed clothes, and one of them had no less than 10 pairs of gloves. As well as these toys, which were highly expensive and perhaps unique, they had more mundane playthings – they outfitted a mini-ature farm with lead livestock bought at Woolworth's with their pocket money.

Whatever the girls played with, there were usually just the two of them, and, in fact, they were so much separated from others of their age that they caught no childhood diseases. This comparative isolation also explains the closeness they felt to animals. For Elizabeth, at least, these were to be a lifelong passion and, surrounded as she would always be by subservi-ent humans, it is easy to understand the attraction of species that could offer recreation and a sense of friendship without the tiresome complications of deference and protocol. From the age of three she had her own dog, and acquired a pony soon after. She was famously to say that, when she grew up, she wanted to marry a farmer so that she could 'live in the country and have lots of horses and dogs'. She first met a corgi when, at the age of seven, she coveted one owned by Viscount Weymouth. Her family soon had one of its own – Dookie. He was not to remain a bachelor for long, and the addition of Jane would create a canine dynasty that would parallel that of the dogs' owners.

The duke and duchess, who seldom entertained and preferred their own company to that of others, were indulgent with their daughters. They were not noticeably strict and, despite the presence of nannies and governesses, there was about Elizabeth's childhood nothing of the Victorian nursery. Their parents saw them for at least an hour, twice a day, and they took their meals together. The Princesses had the run of the whole house rather than being confined to the top floor. Their parents took a close interest in everything they did.

Their desire was to give their daughters a happy childhood, one that – in the duchesses words – 'they can always look back on'. The Duke, cowed by a boisterous father and a more extrovert elder brother, had endured a painful childhood and wanted his own offspring to be much happier. The duchess came from a close, affectionate family and had grown up to be dutiful without the need for strict discipline. She saw to it that the lives of her daughters, as far as was possible, mirrored her own, with the same books and games and interests. Once they were old enough for school, there was no discussion of sending them to one. It was not only that there were no family precedents for such a move, but also that their parents were simply not willing to part with them.

Queen Mary devised a curriculum. She considered it unnecessary for them to learn much about arithmetic, since there would be little need for that. They must, of course, have a great deal of history, as well as knowing something of current affairs. In addition to *The Children's Newspaper*, they therefore read *Punch*, whose beautifully drawn cartoons in those days were a joy to look at – and *The Times*. They had lessons in the Bible and poetry to learn. She chose for them a number of suitable books, children's classics with which they should be acquainted. Elizabeth's favourite, understandably, was *Black Beauty*. There was singing, drawing and painting, and needlework – although Elizabeth made little progress with this. As with Victorian princesses half a century earlier, there was no need to take formal education too seriously. So long as they had good manners, and were armed with a few 'accomplishments', there was no requirement for much further general education.

It was not an onerous system. There was no question of intensive learning, nor of exams looming at any time in the future. Each lesson lasted only half an hour, and every afternoon was free for playing or walks or some educational outing. The girls were taught six days a week, however, so on Saturdays they used an improvised schoolroom at Royal Lodge. In London their classes took place in a small chamber off their parents' sitting room.

Their governess, appointed in 1933, was Miss Marion Crawford. A Scot, she had been recruited from an aristocratic family, and one of her qualifications was that she liked to walk long distances. Nicknamed 'Crawfie' by Elizabeth, she was to stay with the girls throughout their upbringing and to spend the war years with them at Windsor. She became greatly attached to her charges, and the Family in turn treated her as a confidante, but after she left their employ to marry she was to commit the terrible sin of writing about her experiences. She published two books, in 1950 and 1953. The first, *The Little Princesses*, was an anecdotal account of the girls' childhood. The second, *Happy and Glorious*, describe Elizabeth's life before coming to the throne. Although the subject is clearly treated from her particular perspective, the picture she gives of the whole family is an affectionate one. They are largely sympathetic portrayals of the Yorks both before and after the Duke became King, and they provide a wealth of information on the domestic lives of the girls. The books outraged the Family but did more than a little to increase its popularity. They have been extensively mined by historians – they are the only detailed record available of the Princesses' girlhood – but the Family never forgave the author for this breach of privacy.

Riding continued to be the girls' passion. Not only did the Princesses increase their collection of toy horses, but they also learned to handle real ones. Elizabeth, at the age of four, had been taught to ride on the orders of King George by his stud-groom. The child was a very willing pupil and regarded her teacher, Owen, with respectful awe. She rapidly gained from him a detailed knowledge of tack and saddlery and feed, and these things became her chief topic of conversation. The Princesses were also given the use of a pony cart that had belonged to Queen Alexandra. Even when they were in London, they had the opportunity to see horses at close quarters, for the Royal Mews was a short walk away. They would often ask the grooms: 'Please may we go and talk to the horses?'

As can be seen, Elizabeth was the product of an extremely happy and close-knit background. She and Margaret grew up in a sheltered environment, surrounded by deference and overwhelming parental love, able to indulge to the full their passion for pets and countryside, able to avoid school subjects that did not interest them, and unquestioning of their position or the peculiar circumstances that went with it. Their parents deliberately sought to give them an idyllic childhood, rather than one that would fit them for life through rigorous training, discipline and competition, as tended to be the practice with princes.

To further their education, the girls went on a series of expeditions by their grandmother and others. To let them experience the everyday life of the capital they were taken by Miss Crawford on the Underground to Tottenham Court Road, where they had tea at the YWCA – though they were recognised and had to be rescued from a curious crowd by their detective. Although this sounds a mundane enough interlude, it had needed to be planned far ahead, like everything they did, and it would have been for them a considerable expedition. They enjoyed the novelty of handling money, a thing they almost never did, and of figuring out what the different coins were worth.

They went to see the Royal Mint, and visited the great repositories of culture – Hampton Court, the British Museum, Madame Tussaud's (where Elizabeth's wax effigy sat on a pony) and the Victoria and Albert. In this latter they would have seen the gallery of plaster casts of statues and monuments. The striking full-sized naked figure of Michelangelo's David is among them. To this day, visitors who go round to the back of its plinth will see, in a frame, an appropriately sized plaster fig-leaf that was always put on the statue when it was known that Queen Mary was going to visit. The princesses' upbringing was sheltered indeed. Their memories of these trips were dominated by the upright figure of their grandmother, sailing ahead of them to point things out while they attempted to keep up.

The placid life led by the girls was to be shattered, suddenly, when their Uncle David abdicated the throne on 10 December 1936. They had learned very little of the unfolding crisis, and discovered its full implications only on the day that their father succeeded his brother, for Elizabeth saw in the hall a letter left for 'Her Majesty the Queen' and asked: 'That's Mummy now, isn't it?'. Margaret, now also aware of the implications, asked her sister if she would be the next queen. 'Yes,' said Elizabeth, 'some day.' 'Poor you!' replied Margaret.

Elizabeth was aware of the concern of both her parents, and perhaps of her father's outright horror at the prospect that was opening up before him. She heard her mother say: 'We must take what is coming to us and make the best of it. There are going to be great changes.' One of these was the removal of the family to Buckingham Palace ('You mean for ever?' asked Elizabeth when told), a home that no generation of Royals seems to like. It is vast, gloomy, uncomfortable and easy to get lost in. Although only across the road from their old house, it seemed a world away.

Nevertheless, it cast a spell over the sisters. While their grandfather was alive it would have been an intimidating place. Now it belonged to their parents, and could be properly explored without the need to be well behaved. No child could inherit such a kingdom and be unimpressed. There were lengthy corridors – on which they could ride their tricycles – mysterious stairs, cellars and an entire inner quadrangle. The Throne Room, let alone the Ballroom, must have inspired awe. The gardens were vast, not overlooked, and entirely private – though they offered glimpses of the passing world. Best of all, the Royal Mews with their stalls and placid, munching horses were only yards away. It really must have been a huge adventure. The girls lined up their equine toys in the passageway outside their second-floor suite of rooms, although the King had their rocking horse put outside his study so that he could hear the sounds of his children romping. This may have been some compensation for the fact that their parents, and particularly their father, could no longer give them the attention to which they had been accustomed.

Once the Duke became King, Elizabeth's position naturally also changed. She was now second in line to the throne. It is said that from then on she prayed every night for a brother to supersede her. The recent crisis was banished from conversation as if it had not happened. The Family was now fixed upon its new destiny. Elizabeth had undergone a basic education in royal behaviour. Now she was to be schooled specifically for her future tasks. Her father, as a second son, had had no training to be anything but a naval officer. He had been – and remained – terrified of the prospect of ruling. His father, George V, had also been a second son and had experienced a similar naval career. His grandfather, Edward VII, had been deliberately kept from taking any part in affairs of state, and as a result had led a sybaritic, largely unproductive life until he succeeded at the age of 64. The new King was determined that his own successor would not come to the throne with such a lack of relevant experience. There was no recent precedent for the education of a female heir to the throne. The boys of previous generations had simply been packed off into the Navy or given vague courses of education with tutors and at universities. The King himself took on the task of instructing Elizabeth in the performance of a monarch's duties, and a famous photograph, taken when Elizabeth was aged 16, captures this passing on of experience. It shows the King at his desk with his daughter looking over his shoulder as he explains a document from his dispatch box. This image perfectly captures the sense of close association between father and daughter, between the monarchs of the present and future.

She not only learned about administration but also about standing for long hours without getting tired, and never looking peevish, unhappy, tearful or bored. All her life she had seen her relations going about their duty – waving to crowds, greeting, taking salutes, inspecting people or places. She absorbed this subconsciously and found that she could do it too.

Another point was perhaps unspoken but obvious: while her father and grandmother offered examples of how a monarch should behave, her Uncle David – by now in exile on the Continent – showed how the job should not be done. As Prince of Wales he had been famous for a magnetic charm, and this had made many friends for the monarchy during his overseas tours. There had always, however, been stories of his petulance, self-indulgence and downright rudeness to mar the image that his subjects wished to have of him. As monarch for a few months in 1936 he was too preoccupied with Mrs Simpson to give his full attention to matters of state. He proved an extremely half-hearted sovereign, brusquely impatient with the trappings – and obligations – of his position and of the dedication and efforts of those who served him. When he decided to give up the throne, the disappointment with him felt by many in the Empire turned to resentment and hostility. Elizabeth had always been fond of him. He had been a frequent visitor to the Yorks and an indulgent uncle to the girls, who had been gratified by his interest in them (every Christmas he gave Elizabeth one of A. A. Milne's books), although they had seen much less of him since he became King and his personal life grew more complicated. Now Elizabeth saw the effect of his selfishness on her family, the monarchy and the public. Queen Mary never forgave him. Her parents' lives seemed ruined. The Crown appeared to be at its most unpopular since the years of Victoria's seclusion. Perhaps some of the determination to be above reproach that has guided Queen Elizabeth has been the result of witnessing this upheaval.

Before the ink was even dry on the Instrument of Abdication, Queen Mary had begun to take a more detailed interest in the education of her eldest granddaughter. From now on, no child produced by the Duke of Windsor – as he was now styled – would be of any importance. Elizabeth's thoughts and energies, as well as those of the people around her, must be focused on preparing her urgently for the future. Queen Mary sent for the girls' curriculum, studied it and made important changes. There was to be much more history, and there was more learning and reciting of poetry, since it encouraged a feel for the power and rhythm of words, and trained the memory. The lessons would now grow longer, which was appropriate anyway, since the girls were getting older.

Elizabeth herself was naturally conscious of the new mood around her. She was galvanised to pay even greater attention in the classroom, to strain even harder to meet the expectations of family and public. 'I will be good,' she vowed, repeating – consciously or otherwise – word-for-word a statement made 100 years earlier by Princess Victoria.

An imaginative and curious child, she was captivated by the past ('History is so *thrilling!*' she once enthused). It is perhaps not difficult to see the relevance of the subject when it deals so much with your own ancestors, when you are surrounded by their portraits and their possessions, and when you know that you yourself are likely to play some role in the continuing story of the nation. Marion Crawford described looking with her at the portrait of Queen Elizabeth in the Royal Library at Windsor, which had once been the Queen's bedchamber. 'Sometimes,' she recalled, 'my stories were told on the very scene of the historic events I described.' As her predecessor, Princess Victoria, had been in childhood, Princess Elizabeth was fascinated by the figure of the great queen. She even learned by heart Elizabeth's speech to her troops at Tilbury. The girls were also able to use the Royal collections for their education. Every week Miss Crawford had some piece from the picture store sent up to the schoolroom for them to study.

Elizabeth loved the ceremonies, the costumes and the music that went with state occasions and which were the very embodiment of history. This was particularly noticeable in the months before her father's Coronation in the summer of 1937, for this event meant the assembling of all the splendidly costumed officials of which the United Kingdom has so many. Once again, she knew her place in the hierarchy of the Court, and the functions that her parents and grandmother would fulfil. She knew the titles of office-holders and the names of foreign royalty who were coming to stay for the occasion (she reprimanded Miss Crawford for failing to recognise, and curtsy to, King Haakon of Norway in the gardens of Buckingham

Palace). Once again, it was not difficult to be enchanted by the glitter of ceremonial when you yourself were part of it, when you knew so many of those involved, and when any of them would answer your questions. It was also rather head-turning to be able to command the resources of the monarchy. When Princess Elizabeth was 13 her favourite musical was *Rose Marie*. On her birthday she asked the band of the Scots Guards to play tunes from it at Windsor.

The King, knowing that his eldest daughter might well have her own Coronation within a decade or two, used the occasion to teach her about the ceremony, its participants and its significance. He had a picture book created that showed the event from beginning to end, and went through it with her. Queen Mary, too, found a guide to the Coronation procession, this time a relic from the reign of Victoria, and similarly explained the names and functions of the people depicted. Their present-day counterparts could be introduced to the children as they came to the Palace to attend rehearsals. The king was, in any case, given to discussing with her affairs of state, and it was observed that he spoke to her as to an equal.

Elizabeth had already, as a small girl, learned how to wave to crowds. She had understood all her life that people wanted to see her, and that it was a kindness to make herself visible. Gradually, during the 1930s, she became more noticeable at Royal occasions. She was a bridesmaid at the wedding of her uncle, the Duke of Kent, in 1934. She participated in the celebrations for her grandfather's Silver Jubilee. In May 1937, she attended her father's Coronation. She began accompanying her father to events, such as the opening of the National Maritime Museum, and she made a speech in French to welcome the future French President René Coty, as well as greeting other Coronation guests.

Elizabeth took a sisterly interest in Margaret and hoped she would behave ('she *is* rather young for a coronation'). She told her that, in the Abbey: 'If you see someone in a funny hat, you are *not* to point at it and laugh.'

The ceremony itself took place on 12 May 1937. Elizabeth was encouraged to write a journal of the event, and she did so with characteristic thoroughness. On lined paper she wrote neatly in pencil: 'The Coronation, 12 May 1937. To Mummy and Papa. From Lilibet By Herself.' It is preserved in the Royal Archives. It describes the noise of the crowds outside the Palace early that morning, and how the sisters – not yet dressed – watched them through the windows. She writes of the carriage-drive to the Abbey, and the splendour, colour and monotony within. She watched, very solemnly (judging by photographs), the whole of the lengthy and complex ceremony, and appeared with her parents and sister afterward on the Palace balcony to greet the crowds. She and Margaret seemed, in their velvet trains and coronets, straight out of a fairy tale.

Soon afterwards she reached the age at which her contemporaries were beginning secondary school, and her own education took a further step forward. It was arranged that she should take lessons in constitutional history from the Vice Provost of Eton. Henry Marten was amiably professorial, charming and – after teaching generations of boys the complexities of Britain's past and present – extremely capable. The *History of England*, of which he was co-author, was a seminal text-book. The Princess visited him twice weekly in company with Miss Crawford, who had no role in this process but that of observer. They sat in his untidy, book-filled study – where he kept a tame raven – while he expatiated on the mysteries of this subject. He had never taught a girl pupil, and had a tendency based on long habit to address her as 'Gentlemen'. Like her father and grandfather, she was taken exhaustively through that bible of monarchy, Walter Bagehot's *English Constitution*. Although published in 1867, it was as relevant as ever, and her son would one day study it in turn. Elizabeth, always diligent, took copious notes on the green-covered exercise books that were used by the schoolboys while her governess was invited by the affable Marten to relax with a novel.

These sessions may not sound much like a formal education, but they were of immense value. The heir to the throne received, through them, one-to-one tuition specifically tailored to her own circumstances and future from a man who was perhaps the most gifted history teacher of his generation. She studied Trevelyan's *English Social History* and G. R. Elton's *Imperial Commonwealth*. Her tutor discoursed on disparate aspects of law, on the role of Parliament and on economics. To teach her about international affairs he produced an umbrella that opened into a map of the world. To deal with constitutional matters he invented a sort of jigsaw, each piece of which represented some office-holder or aspect of the state, and made the whole subject comprehensible. He must have won her affection not only for his endearing battiness but because he was a great admirer of her heroine Queen Victoria. With her powerful memory, the Princess retained a lot of what she was taught and she was set homework, which, if it was not good enough, might be marked 'N', for nonsense.

The lessons continued for years. When the Princess was at Birkhall on the Balmoral estate, he posted her lessons to her. Once she was at Windsor after the war had begun, he carried his books up to the Castle and taught her there. Princess Margaret was not offered the opportunity to have tutorials with Marten. It was, she was told, 'not necessary'. With the return of peace, he was to be knighted for his services. The ceremony took place in School Yard, Eton's imposing quadrangle, in front of the assembled boys. He deserved this accolade, for he had done his job well. As Queen Elizabeth, his pupil has genuinely impressed advisors and politicians with her absolute command of constitutional matters. She was thoroughly grounded in the things she needed to know.

Elizabeth was aged 13 when, in the summer of 1939 and a matter of weeks away from war, she experienced one of the most significant moments in her life. On 22 June she visited Britannia Royal Naval College at Dartmouth with her parents and sister. They arrived aboard the Royal Yacht, *Victoria and Albert*. The King was a former cadet and, although he had not shone there, he was happy to show his family around the buildings and grounds, where his elder daughter was to plant a tree. Elizabeth and Margaret were not allowed to visit the College itself, owing to an outbreak of mumps, and were instead sent to the home of the Captain (Commanding Officer) where they had somehow to be entertained for several hours. A young cadet, Prince Philip of Greece, who was the nephew of the king's cousin, 'Dickie' Countbatten, was given the task, and he did not relish the company of two small girls. They played for a short while with the train set of the Captain's son, and then Philip suggested they go to a nearby tennis court, where he showed off by jumping over the net. After a tea at which he put away a gargantuan amount of shrimps, the visit came to an end. *Victoria and Albert* steamed out of Dartmouth Harbour accompanied by a fleet of small craft manned by members of the College. Most turned back once in the choppier waters of the open sea, but a single boat continued relentlessly to follow until the King became annoyed at the danger in which its occupant was placing himself. Philip – for it was he – had to be ordered by loud-hailer to return.

This story has passed into legend. It was first recounted by Miss Crawford, who was present. Elizabeth was deeply impressed by Philip's handsome appearance, his athletic ability and his brash self-confidence, so much at odds with her own more reserved nature. Whether or not the details are correct, there can be no doubt that at some time in the months and years that followed she fell seriously in love with him.

# WARTIME, 1939–1947

'Poor Darlings, they have not had any fun yet.'

'Who is this Hitler, spoiling everything?' Princess Margaret had asked. Elizabeth knew, and hated him. She was disappointed when war did not break out in 1938 over Czechoslovakia and was rebuked by her nurserymaid, Miss MacDonald: '*You* don't know what war is like!' When it did come the following year, she found out soon enough. Just over a month later, some 800 men were killed when HMS *Royal Oak* was sunk by a U-boat. Her anguish, and outrage, were genuine: 'It can't be! All those nice sailors!'

The Second World War was to cost the young Princess very heavily. It destroyed the house in which she was born, the chapel in which she was christened, the home she had loved for the first decade of her life. Her parents were almost killed; her uncle was. She herself heard the sound of falling bombs and anti-aircraft fire, and had to go to shelter when enemy planes were overhead. She saw a doodlebug crash and explode in Windsor Great Park (more than 300 bombs fell there during the conflict). She would perhaps see – and would at least hear –

the waves of German bombers passing over the Castle on their way to annihilate Coventry. She worried about her father when he put himself in danger by travelling to war-zones, and about her 'young man', serving in convoys on the North Sea, the Atlantic and the Pacific. She experienced rationing and shortages (even Royalty had a black line painted round its baths to prevent overfilling). She suffered separation from her parents.

On the outbreak of war, in September 1939, the princesses were at Balmoral, and remained there. For the time being, their idyll continued. 'Are we too happy?' the conscience-stricken girl was to ask when the war eventually became more serious and more dangerous. Although initially nothing happened, for Hitler was still digesting Poland, there was the danger of air raids. Since the previous year, when war had almost begun, extensive precautions had been taken to protect both buildings and people. There were air-raid drills, wardens and auxiliary medical services, concrete shelters, sandbags everywhere. The contents of museums were removed to safety. There was much talk of sending people abroad, too. It was speculated that the princesses might go to Canada to wait out hostilities.

King George would not consider this. He would not be parted from his daughters, and saw it as important to national morale that the Royal Family stay in Britain. It was decided, however, that some members should depart from London. Queen Mary went to stay at Badminton, the country house in Gloucestershire, where she was to pass the war years very happily. The girls would live at Royal Lodge for the time being, for the house should be safe enough from aerial attack, and amid familiar surroundings it was hoped that their lives could retain at least a modicum of normality. The King and Queen lived largely at Buckingham Palace, feeling that it was important to remain in the capital and share whatever dangers were to come. They spoke to the princesses by telephone at six o'clock every evening but saw them only at weekends, which they spent at Windsor. Both the sovereign and his consort practised shooting with rifles and pistols and, when travelling, the King sometimes carried a sten gun. Should the Germans invade, the Queen declared that: 'I shall not go down like the others.' The monarchies of Belgium and Denmark were trapped by the invaders when German forces overran western Europe in May 1940. Those of Norway and the Netherlands had to flee. The British monarchy was determined to fight. Even Queen Mary toted a pistol.

And there were some dangerous moments. In September 1940, two days after the start of the Blitz, a bomb fell on the Palace. It did not explode and the King carried on working in his study above it. It *did* blow up the next day, destroying the swimming-pool that had only recently been built. While this attack might have been random, there was another one exactly a week later that was intentional. The Palace was extremely conspicuous from the air, and a raider flew calmly up the Mall to drop a total of six bombs, which landed in the forecourt, the quadrangle, the chapel and the garden. For the King and Queen to stay in London was more than a mere gesture. They were risking their lives as much as any Londoners.

Meanwhile the girls helped collect scrap metal for the war effort and, like all children living in the country at that time, they helped with the harvesting of fruit and vegetables. They made donations from their pocket money to help the Red Cross. Elizabeth made a gallant attempt to knit items of clothing for soldiers – this was something the aged Queen Victoria had done during the Boer War – but the experiment was not a success.

After the fall of France in the summer of 1940, there was a real possibility of German invasion. The girls were moved for safety from Royal Lodge into the Castle itself. Britain is a peaceful country, and its castles had not had to provide shelter against enemies for several centuries. Now, in a sense, Windsor once again became a fortress rather than a palace. Isolated on its hilltop amid extensive grounds, it was almost impossible for enemy bombers to miss had they wished to make a serious or extensive raid on it. Nearby reservoirs could have enabled a landing by seaplanes. The Park provided a perfect setting for a parachute drop. Despite its massive walls, Windsor therefore did not always seem very safe and its grounds were patrolled with grim purpose at night by soldiers and Home Guard.

From behind its battlements the raids on London, or Slough, were clearly audible and would have made a deep impression on the princesses. They must also have felt considerable sorrow when their old house in Piccadilly was hit. The war would have seemed a very personal matter when their parents' home, Buckingham Palace, was bombed by the Luftwaffe.

On a number of occasions the sirens sent them down to the Castle's dungeons, one of which had been prepared as a shelter. The first time this happened, there was sudden concern when the princesses and their nanny failed to appear. Minutes went by and Sir Hill Child, the Master of the Household, was beside himself with anxiety. Miss Crawford, the governess, called up the stairs of the Brunswick Tower, in which the girls had their quarters: 'What are you doing?'

'We're dressing,' replied Elizabeth.

This was taking propriety too far. Child made it clear that in future there must be no such delays. The thought of the heir to the throne being killed because she, or her dresser, felt she should have her shoes properly tied was something he did not want on his conscience. When the all-clear sounded, however, his natural courtesy at once returned: 'You may go to bed now, Ma'am,' he told Elizabeth, bowing.

With practice, a routine was established. The girls had bunks in the shelter, suitcases packed with both essentials and sentimental treasures, and 'siren-suits' – as popularised by the Prime Minister – to enable them to be dressed in seconds. However successful he was at getting the girls to cooperate, Child was to find their mother more difficult to convince. The Queen, when the siren dragged them all out of bed, simply refused to be hurried into behaving in a flustered or undignified manner. She not only dressed completely for the shelter but did so with deliberate slowness, as a point of honour. After a while she decided not to bother going below ground at all, regarding it as being too much trouble, and announced that they would take their chances above ground.

Against this background of enemy action, the Buckingham Palace Guide Troop, founded for the princesses and their friends, had transferred to Windsor where they carried on their activities, though now they were drilled by a Sergeant Major of the Grenadiers. They held a camp in the Park, but there could be no doubt that this was not an ordinary troop – tents were erected for them by Guardsmen and their food was provided by the Castle pantries. The unit contained a number of evacuee girls from working-class districts in London. Margaret was better at mixing with them than her sister who, with her trade-mark shyness already in evidence, found an excuse to sleep on her own in a nearby summer house rather than under canvas. Elizabeth was promoted to Patrol Leader.

On 13 October 1940, Princess Elizabeth, then 14 years old, broadcast to the children of the Empire on the radio programme *Children's Hour*. Coached in delivery, and with her mother beating time, the Princess said in a measured and confident voice: 'My sister Margaret Rose and I feel so much for you, for we too know from experience what it means to be away from those we love most of all.' She ended on an upbeat: 'We know, every one of us, that in the end all shall be well.' Princess Margaret, at her elbow, was urged to join her in wishing her audience farewell: 'Good night, and good luck to you all.' Its target audience was the juvenile diaspora that had been scattered by evacuation, and especially those fortunate enough to have been sent to North America – a sad separation but a comfortable exile. It was a well-delivered speech that has remained fixed in the national memory. Together with the talk she was to broadcast on her 21st birthday, it was among the most memorable of all the hundreds the Queen has given. One who heard it was the South African writer Sarah Gertrude Millin, who was moved to remark: 'If there are still queens in the world a generation hence, this child will be a good queen.'

Windsor was a most agreeable place in which to sit out these years of confinement. The Castle and parks were, of course, full of beauty and interest, and were peaceful most of the time. There were also interesting and talented people wherever one looked, either resident or passing through. Household regiments were rotated throughout the war as they were in peacetime, bringing a changing series of high-spirited young officers and imposing, respectful Guardsmen. There were courtiers with a sense of fun, such as Sir Hill Child. Although he may have wrung his hands over the princesses' slowness in dressing, he took them into the Castle cellars to show them where the Crown Jewels were hidden, wrapped in newspaper.

There were also local teachers who were willing to help maintain morale. One of them, Hubert Tanner, was headmaster of the little local school in the Park. He produced, for Christmas 1940, a nativity play that was performed by local children, evacuees and ... the princesses. Both girls delighted in the experience, and the following year a more ambitious undertaking was attempted. This was a pantomime – *Cinderella* – with sophisticated costumes, and original music by Mr Tanner (who also acted in the productions) that was staged in the Castle's Waterloo Chamber. It perhaps goes without saying that the two princesses had the lead roles – but then a major purpose was to train the girls towards confidence in public – with Elizabeth as Prince Charming and her sister as Cinderella herself. Here Margaret, who all her life would enjoy singing, had her first taste of applause. Her audience was made up of local people, estate workers, soldiers and the families of Castle staff. Tickets were sold in aid of something called the Royal Household Knitting Wool Fund. Their parents enjoyed themselves hugely, the King, who had a simple and hearty sense of humour, laughing loudly throughout. This was precisely the sort of golden memory on which he wanted his daughters to be able to look back. His own shyness having never left him, he was gratified to see that his heir could appear in public with such lack of inhibition.

The performances became an annual tradition. *Aladdin* was put on the next year, and was followed by a show whose title – *Old Mother Red Riding Boots* – suggests a rather tongue-in-cheek concoction based on several children's stories. For the princesses these productions, with their elaborate costumes and serving soldiers drafted in as extras, were an important part of their lives. The Queen took them as seriously as any indulgent parent, going over the scripts with them, testing them on their lines and cues. A frisson of excitement was added during *Aladdin* by the presence in the audience of Philip, on leave from the Navy.

This was not the only distraction. Many years after the war, the author A. N. Wilson was to sit next to the Queen Mother at luncheon. In the course of their conversation she recalled that, because during the war she felt her daughters were missing out on culture, a poetry evening was arranged. T. S. Eliot came to the Castle and read his best-known work. Her Majesty recalled: 'We had this rather lugubrious man in a suit, and he read a poem. I think it was called "The Desert". And first the girls got the giggles, and then I did and then even the King.'

'"The Desert", Ma'am?' replied Wilson. 'Are you sure you don't mean "The Waste Land"?'

'That's it. I'm afraid we all giggled. Such a gloomy man, looked as though he worked in a bank, and we didn't understand a word.'

Wilson repeated this exchange in an article for *The Spectator*, and faced a good deal of censure for disclosing a private conversation with a member of the Royal Family. Surely no one could object, however, to an anecdote that shows such good-natured humour, and offers such a delightful glimpse of their lives?

Further afield, the Royal Family lost its first member on active service for centuries. Prince George, Duke of Kent – the King's youngest surviving brother – had been serving in the RAF. Elizabeth had been a bridesmaid at his wedding in 1934. Like numerous other young men in that branch of service, he was tragically killed not in action but in a flying accident. In August 1942, while travelling over Scotland to Iceland aboard a Sunderland flying boat to inspect bases, his plane collided with a mountainside in thick fog. Wartime air travel was highly risky. The King, on two occasions, flew overseas to visit theatres of operations. Both times he returned without mishap, but his family had been extremely concerned.

The Princess's training for her future role became increasingly serious. Although by 1942 the threat from German bombers had receded, there was to be another Blitz two years later when the V-1 and V-2 rockets began to fall on England. During this, her parents again remained in London. The King was well aware that, by courting danger, he was increasing the risk that his daughter might suddenly become queen, and that she must be as prepared as possible. She was, in any case, reaching young adulthood and it would not be long before she began to assume some royal duties.

For the time being, her only official position was that of Sea Ranger. She had graduated to this after passing out of the Guides on reaching 16. On her birthday that year she went, as did all young women of her age, to a Labour Exchange to register for work under the Wartime Youth Service Scheme. She longed to do something useful, and relished having this experience in common with others of her age, but it was no more than a gesture. The King refused to let her be assigned any form of duty, believing that she was already helping the war effort by keeping up morale through her membership of the Royal Family. He did not want the heir to the throne to be, as it were, out of reach. As the Head-of-State-in-waiting, she must remain close at hand. He found her a position that was more suitable.

Her father appointed her Colonel of the Grenadier Guards. She took the salute at a parade on her birthday, and the Colonel's Colour that she received was, understandably, the 'present' she most appreciated. The previous Colonel, who had just died, had been the Duke of Connaught. Born in 1850, son of Victoria and godson of Wellington, he had been a professional soldier all his life. There can have been no greater contrast with a vivacious schoolgirl – she was the youngest-ever Colonel-in-Chief in the British Army – yet he would have had no fault to find with her bearing or her enthusiasm. The men themselves must have looked upon her appointment as a breath of fresh air.

In the drab and austere war years the regiment, like all others, had had to lay aside the visual splendour that charac-terised its public appearances in peacetime; nevertheless, she was delighted. The Princess was anxious to do something useful towards the war effort and, though in any case still too young to serve, this gave her a personal connection with an illustrious military unit. She was proud to wear its grenade badge in her hat. There was certainly nothing schoolgirlish about her involvement with the regiment. At the parade she stood ramrod-straight and solemn-faced, and when inspecting the men found fault with details to such an extent that she had to be tactfully asked to show less zeal. It may seem likely that, given her sheltered upbringing, Philip of Greece was the only man she had had opportunity of meeting or getting to know. In fact, Windsor was full of charming and suitable young Guards officers, many of them from families known to her parents, and her connection with the Grenadiers brought her especially close to some of them. She followed their fortunes throughout the war, and was to count some of them – such as Lord Porchester, who became her Racing Manager – as life-long friends.

And it was at this same age that she discovered the pleasures of racing. She was taken by the King to Wiltshire to watch his trainer exercising horses on the Downs. A lifetime of interest in horses of any sort was suddenly compounded by the sight of these thoroughbreds in training, and added a new dimension to the pony-club affection she had had as a girl. She met a jockey – Gordon Richards – and was introduced to a world of equine specialists and experts whose manner, speech and knowledge she found fascinating. She was, remarkably quickly, to match their expertise. She visited the Royal Stud soon afterwards, establishing a connection that has continued ever since. Her father had been a nominal race-goer; his daughter would make up for his lack of fervour.

A further step was taken towards her future position when Parliament amended legislation so that, as soon as she was 18, she could become a Councillor of State and deputise for the King when his visits to battlefronts took him away from Britain. She would otherwise not have been eligible until she was 21.

Although devoted to her parents and willing to be guided by her elders, Elizabeth possessed a good deal of stubbornness. If she wanted something badly enough she was capable of fighting for it. By the beginning of 1945 the conflict, in Europe at least, was clearly not going to last much longer. She still yearned to have some sort of active role in the war effort and badgered her father to grant his permission to enlist. He eventually yielded and allowed her to join the Armed Forces. As heir to the throne she would have been a prize catch for any of the women's services, and these had an informal hierarchy of prestige. The WRNS (Women's Royal Naval Service) was at the top, followed by the WRAF (Women's Royal Air Force) and the WRAC (Women's Royal Army Corps). Last in this pecking order was the ATS (Auxiliary Territorial Service), a unit whose functions included the decidedly unglamorous occupation of vehicle-maintenance. Elizabeth joined this – and was to be proud for the rest of her life of the mechanical and driving skills it gave her. She was commissioned as Second Subaltern (lieutenant) Princess Elizabeth, Army number 20873, and attached to No. 1 Mechanical Transport Training Centre near Camberley – a place sufficiently near Windsor to make commuting possible. She was fitted for her khaki uniform, and polished the buttons herself!

This would undoubtedly have been a chance to live a relatively ordinary life, had it been taken. The Princess, however, did not share all the experiences of her contemporaries. On the first day of service she was collected from Windsor by her commanding officer. Thereafter – at the insistence of the King, who had made this a condition – she returned home every evening to dine and sleep, leaving again after breakfast to be driven to camp. Servants pressed her uniforms. Although she shared the duties of her unit, acting as officer of the day when her turn came, she did not mingle with the others. At lectures she came into the room last and left it first, always occupying the middle of the front row and flanked by senior officers. No one addressed her as anything other than 'Ma'am' or 'Your Royal Highness', though the girls had little chance to talk to her anyway. Yet she was as curious about them as they must have been about her. Whenever one of them asked a question in a lecture, the Princess would turn in her seat and stare at them, anxious to recognise faces and learn names. A rare and useful glimpse of Royalty from the other side was afforded her, however, when she had to help prepare the camp for a visit by the Princess Royal, her aunt. She later fumed: 'What a business it has been. Spit and polish all day long. Now I know what goes on when Mummy and Papa go anywhere.'

She completed the course in vehicle maintenance, but in the process she had become obsessed, as people do when a new interest takes up all their time, with technicalities. The fact that her parents knew nothing about these matters may have added to her pleasure in mastering the subject. 'We had sparking-plugs last night all through dinner,' her mother famously sighed. The King and Queen attended her graduation, and no doubt were as proud as she was.

As well as learning to repair engines, the Princess perfected her ability to drive. She had already taken lessons in Windsor Great Park, and had been given a Daimler by the King for her 18th birthday. She took her test by driving her commanding officer to Buckingham Palace from Aldershot. This involved negotiating London's traffic – no small thing even in those relatively uncrowded days – and going twice round Piccadilly Circus.

She began to take a structured, rather than occasional, part in public duties. She acted as hostess to visiting military and political leaders, visited camps and bases, inspected troops, and even travelled in secret to watch a rehearsal for the parachute drop that would take place on D-Day.

As evidence that she had now joined the adult world, Elizabeth was given her own rooms in Buckingham Palace – a bedroom, dressing room, bathroom and sitting room that overlooked the Mall. She was also given two members of staff – a housemaid and footman. Within a few months of her birthday she was to perform the duty of Councillor of State, signing the reprieve for a murderer. She would also attend a luncheon at Guildhall and make a public speech for the first time.

There was some speculation about whether she should have a further title. 'Princess Elizabeth' was still associated in the public mind with the small girl surrounded by dogs and horses. Could she not, it was pondered, celebrate her coming of age by being created Princess of Wales? The King, who was a stickler for protocol, would not hear of it. That title was only for the wife of the Prince of Wales. Subjects north of the border asked if she could therefore become Princess of Scotland. There was no such title and the monarch did not consider establishing it. The matter was simply forgotten, and his daughter remained Princess Elizabeth until she became queen.

When the war ended in Europe, the family were together in London. Elizabeth joined her parents, and the Prime Minister, on the Palace balcony on 8 May 1945, dressed in her khaki ATS uniform. That evening with the celebrations still going on, they persuaded the King to let them out into the crowd. Once suitable escorts were arranged, he gave consent. 'Poor darlings,' he told the Queen, 'they have not had any fun yet.' After dark, she and Margaret went, with several friends and young officers, incognito into the crowd and joined in the celebrations. They went along the Mall into Piccadilly Circus, unrecognised. They also stood in front of the Palace and joined in the calls for the King and Queen. There was no doubt that this summons would be answered. Their parents knew they would be somewhere outside in the sea of faces, and had been told they must appear!

Three months later the scene was repeated when Japan surrendered. This time Elizabeth stood on the balcony not in uniform but in a summer dress, and she filmed the crowds with a movie camera.

Before the war had ended, Princess Elizabeth had furthered the passion for racing that had begun a few years earlier. In June 1945 she attended races at Newmarket for the first time with her parents. The King's horse, Rising Light, came fifth. Given her long-standing fascination with horses and the impetus this had received from meeting trainers, it was perhaps only to be expected that she would take such an interest in the notion of them, brought to a pitch of beauty and fitness and grace, competing for prizes through their own ability and the skill and empathy of those who rode them. She also experienced the heady sensation of favouring a horse and willing it to win, as well as the pleasure of watching such contests in the company of thousands who shared her enthusiasm – a genuinely democratic crowd made up of all classes, giving her a rare opportunity to participate in a communal activity. Racing had been, of course, a very long tradition in her family – Charles II had been an enthusiastic visitor to Newmarket, and Ascot had been founded by Queen Anne – but no monarch since Edward VII had followed it with great enthusiasm. Now, within a few years, a golden age of royal racing would begin. The Queen Mother was, of course, to become similarly – indeed even more – associated with the sport.

With the war over and the Princess now grown up, there was naturally speculation about whom she would marry. The King was concerned that his daughter had not met enough young men to make a mature judgement regarding her future, and he began to invite to Balmoral, Sandringham or Ascot young blue-bloods who could give her a broader perspective. Although she enjoyed, as any young girl would, the company of sophisticated people of her own age, it became clear that her heart was already committed.

There could be no questioning her affection for Prince Philip. She had kept his photograph on her desk for years and written to him frequently. She had had to worry about him, for he had been in danger on numerous occasions. He had served in the Mediterranean, where his ship bombarded the Libyan coast and took part in the battle at Cape Matapan. In this action, which had put Italy's surface fleet out of the war, he had manned the searchlights aboard HMS *Valiant*. He was given a Mention in Dispatches that read: 'Thanks to his alertness and appreciation of the situation, we were able to sink in five minutes two Italian cruisers.' He took part in convoys along the east coast of Britain. He crossed the Atlantic, and he was posted to the Pacific where – thanks to his influential uncle – he was aboard USS *Missouri* to witness the signing of the Japanese surrender. In between, however, he had appeared in London several times on leave, or while his ship was being refitted. Elizabeth was clearly delighted to see him. No one could have mistaken her excitement when she found he was coming to *Aladdin* at Windsor. Although they had not been together a great deal, they had seen enough of each other to deepen their friendship significantly.

The Princess and Philip were, to a large extent, an attraction of opposites. Not only were their natures very different, his experiences and hers had very little in common. He was not, like many of her friends among the Guards officers, from a background of landed estates and country pursuits. Nor did he have wealth that would have enabled him to keep pace with the lifestyle of the Royals. He shared none of Elizabeth's passion for the Turf (in later years he was said to disappear into the Royal Box at Ascot and watch cricket on television while the Queen attended to the races). From the perspective of the senior British aristocracy he was an outsider. He was literally homeless, and had nothing to live on except his naval pay, which was £11 a week.

And what were the feelings of the young man himself? Shortly after he had passed out of Dartmouth in the summer before the war began, his uncle contacted an old acquaintance. Vice-Admiral Harold Baillie-Grohman was Captain of the battleship HMS *Ramillies* in the Mediterranean, and Mountbatten requested that his nephew be assigned to the ship. When the young man arrived, he was invited to the Captain's cabin to meet his commanding officer. The Admiral was astonished when, in answer to questions about his future ambitions, Philip said: 'My Uncle Dickie has plans for me. He thinks I could marry Princess Elizabeth.'

'Are you really fond of her?' he was asked.

'Oh, yes, very. I write to her every week.'

The Captain was sufficiently struck by this exchange to write it down verbatim.

In 1941 the diarist Henry 'Chips' Channon met Philip at a cocktail party and recorded matter-of-factly: 'Prince Philip of Greece was there. He is to be our Prince Consort and that is why he is serving in our Navy.' Gossip and rumour had married them off many years before they became engaged.

By the end of the war it was common knowledge throughout the Navy that Philip was to court the Princess. He made no attempt to silence such speculation.

With her role in the Royal family becoming established, and even her hobby now decided upon, it became clear that – in the minds of the Princess and the young naval officer – another important issue had also been settled.

# NEW ERA, 1947–1952

'Poor Lil. Nothing of your own. Not even your love affair.'

With the war over, Princess Elizabeth's public duties became more routine. She now visited towns and factories rather than camps or troops in training, and often carried out these functions in company with her parents or her grandmother. Although young and undeniably pretty, Elizabeth dressed very much like her mother – they had the same dressmaker – and therefore had a tendency to look older than her years. As an emerging public personality she was the focus of considerable interest, and she was even the subject of a film – *Heir to the Throne*. It was to be the first of numerous documentaries that would show the public the nature of her life and work.

The years between 1945 and her accession in 1952 were a brief interlude by the standards of a long life. Within this period she experienced apprenticeship, courtship, marriage and children – a chance to know something approaching normality as well as a relative freedom from responsibility.

But such things were always, and only, relative. She had by now taken on the patronage, or presidency, of several organisations: the RSPCC, the Royal College of Music, the Life Saving Society, the Red Cross, the Student Nurses' Association. She already spent her days answering letters, accepting – or declining – invitations, attending lunches, watching demonstrations of industry or military precision or emergency procedure, and making speeches.

As she settled into this routine of public duties, the qualities that were to characterise her in the future became apparent. She was aware that she lacked her mother's social gifts, and the smiles she offered to crowds and to photographers were bashful and often unsure. It was known by those close to her that she spent an anxious time before dinners wondering who she would sit next to and what she would talk to them about, and she was soon to make a point of reading notes in advance on people in such situations. There is something rather touching about the notion of a 20-year-old practising conversation. Instead of spontaneity and wit she had diligence and a good memory. She sharpened the skills she possessed in order to make up for those she lacked. She was described, tongue-in-cheek, at this stage of her life as being 'like a very healthy, sound, responsible prefect in a boarding school, marked out to be head girl'. Her shyness, in any case, endeared her to her father's subjects.

The matter about which she felt most reticent was Philip. Her feelings for him had not changed, and her determination to marry him was obvious. The King still had difficulty in accepting that she had fallen for him so quickly and so young. His uncle Lord Mountbatten was persistent in pushing his suit, as he had been since the young people had first met. He had been at Dartmouth on the day of the Royal Family's visit, and had taken pains to ensure that his nephew was highly conspicuous. It was he who had arranged for Philip to look after the girls.

Mountbatten was a man of charm and brilliance, but these qualities were almost eclipsed by vanity and ambition. A career naval officer like his father – who had been hounded from office in the First World War because of a German name and background – he was a cousin of the Windsors but his own family (the Battenbergs had anglicised their name) was a very minor and unimportant branch of European royalty, and he passionately wanted to see it grow in prestige and influence. His handsome and personable nephew, with whom he had had few dealings until half-a-dozen years earlier, could be a means of achieving this. The Princess obviously liked Philip but her mother was less impressed. The Queen distrusted Mountbatten, whose motives she recognised, and his sponsorship of Philip did not stand in the young man's favour. Even the candidate himself became alarmed by the vigour with which his uncle seemed to be forcing matters, pleading in a letter: 'Please, I beg of you, not too much advice in an affair of the heart or I shall be forced to do the wooing by proxy.'

If this sounds like some Byzantine plot to capture the throne it is worth remembering that, until within living memory, this is how all dynasties tended to operate. From the time she reached adolescence there had been speculation about Princess Elizabeth's future husband. It would have been entirely natural that possible candidates for the hand of the Princess should be considered. Any suitable young man could have been discussed, and would have had supporters and detractors. Those who knew the Princess and her parents might have made suggestions, perhaps arranging for her to meet someone in order to see how they got on together. This is by no means unusual behaviour among the Queen's subjects, many of whom owe happy marriages to precisely that sort of arranged meeting.

People in the Royal Family were not, as they are today, free to fall in love with ordinary members of the public and marry them. The pool from which a young man could be drawn was by definition very small, for not only were there qualifications of birth but of temperament. Her husband must have credibility with the peoples of the Empire as well as being capable of living a life of unremitting duty. In addition to that, he must actually love her. The days of dynastic marriages – mere political alliances between ruling houses – had ended with the Great War. King George VI, whose own happiness was entirely due to marrying for love, would not have considered letting Elizabeth or Margaret be wed for any other reason. Like any indulgent father he would take a great deal of convincing that *any* young man was good enough for his daughter.

The senior aristocracy was seen as the most likely place to find a husband for the Princess and one or two young dukes – Grafton and Rutland – were discreetly considered, though both were soon to make marriage plans of their own.

The King was fond enough of Philip, whose extrovert nature was in such stark contrast to his own, but a number of his courtiers were not enthusiastic. He was a member of a Royal House but it was not one that was ancient, powerful or stable, and his father – divorced and living hand-to-mouth around Europe – had left an unedifying reputation. Philip himself was the nephew of a marquess – Milford Haven – but showed none of the quiet urbanity that was the ideal of the aristocracy. He had been to a British boarding school but it was not the kind of traditional, top-drawer establishment that would have been taken seriously by courtiers. He obviously had a rebellious streak – it has been suggested that this might have hindered his career had he stayed in the Navy – and officials could sense friction ahead. Again, the fact that Mountbatten, himself something of an outsider, was behind him did his cause little good. He could be blunt and disrespectful toward older people and it was wondered, given his striking looks, overwhelming confidence and social popularity (he enjoyed the friendship of women, and this could be misinterpreted), whether he would be able to resist temptation enough to be a faithful husband. The King's Private Secretary saw him as: 'rough, uneducated and [would] probably [be] unfaithful'.

Philip was to mature into a phlegmatic, often charming but frequently outspoken man. His accent and appearance, his attitudes and his sporting interests all epitomise the English aristocracy. He would come to personify the British Establishment. It is strange to think that he was once disapproved of by that same Establishment for not fitting with its notion of what was proper. Many decades later, when Princess Diana felt harassed by the expectations of senior courtiers, it surprised some people to learn that she had had support from Prince Philip. He, too, had run the gauntlet of snobbish disapproval.

As shown, he had the support of Queen Mary. She had known him since his childhood – she used to invite him to tea at the Palace – and had cherished the hope that he would marry her granddaughter. Although some rough corners might have to be knocked off, she saw in him qualities of drive, energy and confidence that would be useful to the monarchy, a counterbalance to the modesty of her son and granddaughter.

The British public proved surprisingly reluctant to take to him. Once he had been seen in public with the Princess – the first occasion was the wedding of Patricia Mountbatten – the press began to speculate openly. As the question of an engagement hovered, assumed but unspoken and unconfirmed (the Palace kept issuing denials when the matter was raised), there remained a feeling that Elizabeth could do better. However handsome he might be, whatever his war-record might have been, opinion would have preferred that the Princess marry a compatriot. Philip was seen as a foreigner in spite of his education, service and connections. A photograph of him, taken during the war and showing him with a beard (Elizabeth had kept the picture on her desk) was published and in that clean-shaven era it made him look like some Ruritanian grandee and certainly not like a man to be taken seriously. A poll of readers carried out by the *Sunday Pictorial* found that 40 per cent disapproved of a match between them.

Elizabeth would naturally have found it humiliating to have her relationship debated in the national press and, feeling that it was no one's business but her own, she could be nettled if even well-wishers brought up the matter. She was shocked when, during a visit to a factory, someone called out: 'Where's Philip?' 'That was horrible!' she said. 'Poor Lil,' her sister commiserated. 'Nothing of your own. Not even your love affair.'

In the autumn of 1946, Philip was invited to Balmoral. In a sense he, too, was waiting to see what would happen. He has given the impression that the understanding between them gradually deepened into certainty, and perhaps the whole Household was in suspense awaiting the news. The purpose of his stay there was, at least partly, to give him a final and thorough vetting as to his suitability for life in the Royal Family. It has been speculated that there is what is called 'the Balmoral test'. Any prospective spouse who fails to enjoy the spartan surroundings, or the tiring days spent tramping the hills in the rain, will not do. One who immediately passed this had been Elizabeth Bowes-Lyon, while a conspicuous failure was her sister-in-law, Wallis Simpson (on first glimpsing the tartan carpets, she had exclaimed: 'Those will have to go!'). If there is such a test, there was little danger that Philip would be found wanting. As a schoolboy at Gordonstoun he was already accustomed to living in northern Scotland. He was keen on outdoor pursuits, and adapted without difficulty to the shooting-and-stalking culture of Deeside.

Philip and Elizabeth became engaged at some point during those weeks. Royal betrothals are not always secret – we know exactly when and where Victoria proposed to Albert, and even what was said – but in this case both partners have kept the details to themselves.

Yet there was no public announcement. The King wanted to delay the news until after a visit to South Africa that would be made early in 1947. All four members of the immediate Royal

Family were to go, and they would be away for four months. Elizabeth, for the second and last time in her life, collided with the wishes of her parents. The first time, over the issue of joining the ATS, she had got her way, though with a compromise – having to live at home – that robbed the experience of much of its value. Now she wished to marry sooner rather than later. Despite her stubbornness, she gave way to her parents. It cost her some anguish to do so, but she not only accepted her father's request to delay, she also – once she had married and the waiting was over – wrote to the King and told him that he had been right to insist on this. In comparison with the arguments that many young women have with their parents, these *contretemps* seem mild indeed, even though the issues at stake were significant. They show both what a placid and conciliatory nature the Princess had, and what a loving family she belonged to.

Why was the King so intent on secrecy? There were several reasons. First of all, Elizabeth was not yet 21, and the King wanted her to have passed that milestone – to have officially left childhood for adulthood – before the question of her marriage was made public. Secondly, the man she wished to marry was not a British citizen, although he had served in the British Forces. He was in the process of becoming naturalised, but even his Royal connections could not speed up the wheels of bureaucracy, and his papers had not come through until 7 February – after the time the tour had begun (somewhat absurdly he was, through Hanoverian descent, eligible for automatic citizenship all along). Thirdly, the King was a doting parent who did not wish to part with his daughter. He had so greatly valued the compact little unit that was his family that he dreaded its breaking up, and he was to some extent putting off the moment of parting. Fourthly, he wanted to be sure that Elizabeth was certain. Because of her high public profile there could be no mistakes. If she became engaged and then met someone she liked more, there would be very considerable embarrassment. He felt it better if nothing was said for the present. He wanted his daughter to have several months in which to search her heart and see if her fondness was genuine. He knew that the young people wrote to each other continuously and that the public already considered them a couple, but still he resisted. Once the family was home a decision could be made.

Following the First World War, the then Prince of Wales had made extensive tours of the Empire to thank its member states for their contribution. Something of the same order was envisaged after the Second World War, but not as a sweep through an entire hemisphere or chain of countries. On this occasion the Royal Family would visit only one Dominion – South Africa – and all of them would go. The sovereign himself was suffering the stress of recent years. He needed a rest, and the voyage to the Cape would provide it. His daughters, who had never been outside Britain, were old enough to be shown to his peoples.

For the occasion, Elizabeth and Margaret were given an allotment of extra clothing coupons. Despite the wartime restrictions still in place, it was expected that Royals always be immaculate and wear a variety of costume. One formal dress each would not have sufficed.

They sailed aboard HMS *Vanguard*, the Royal Navy's largest battleship. Elizabeth knew the ship. She had attended its launching when its completion was rushed to enable it to take part in the expected invasion of Japan. The Princess was photographed wearing a feminine version of a sailor's cap with the ship's tally on its band. She and Margaret were also photographed skylarking with young officers on deck, and practising shooting with their parents, lying prone and aiming rifles. Photographs published at home showed the Royals relaxing like any other family on a cruise and the King, whom his subjects were accustomed to seeing in naval uniform, appeared in shorts and knee-socks. As always with the Royal Family, however, there was work to do. In this case it was necessary to rehearse speeches and phrases in Afrikaans, and to study the country's history and culture. The voyage was pleasant – the seas became increasingly warm as they travelled south, and they were escaping a particularly nasty winter at home – but it was not idyllic. Elizabeth was a poor sailor, and suffered on the way through the Bay of Biscay. 'I, for one, would gladly have died,' she wrote afterward. The Princess who during the war had pondered: 'Are we too happy?' felt guilty at being under balmy skies while her father's subjects were suffering sub-zero temperatures, as well as a coal shortage, and her letters home were filled with commiseration and enquiries about conditions. She showed especial concern for the elderly and for those who could not afford adequate heating.

In April, the Princess celebrated her 21st birthday. Her hosts, the government of South Africa, presented her with a necklace of 21 diamonds – which she was shortly to wear at her wedding. She marked the occasion by making the second important radio address of her life, and she prepared for it with customary diligence. She wrote the rough draft during a day's relaxation on the coast. While the King and Princess Margaret swam in the sea, she worked on it under a canvas awning, ignoring the temptation to join them. Later, aboard the royal train, she went over the speech and rehearsed it with her sister as audience. It was very simple: 'I declare before you all that my whole life, whether it be long or short, shall be devoted to your service and the service of the great Imperial Commonwealth to which we all belong. But I shall not have strength to carry out this resolution unless you join in it with me, as I now invite you to do. I know that your support will be unfailingly given. God bless all of you who are willing to share it.' The 'great Imperial Commonwealth' was to get smaller. Before the end of the year, India was to become an independent republic. Burma would, within two years, sever all connections with Britain, and South Africa itself would eventually leave the Commonwealth for an entire generation. Nevertheless, the speech was highly impressive. The words were tidied up by the King's Private Secretary but the sentiments had been her own. They were sincerely held and have guided her ever since. They have been frequently quoted, and indeed make up the Queen's most well-known speech. The young woman who had been thrilled by her namesake's address to the troops at Tilbury had now uttered stirring and memorable words of her own. It is said that she herself was moved to tears when reading the final draft.

And there were noble gestures as well as words. In Basutoland she and Margaret inspected several hundred Girl Guides. Afterward she asked if they had seen all of those who had come for the event. Apparently they had not, for there was a busload of leper girls nearby. The Princess immediately asked to meet them. Taking Margaret, she went over and greeted them, making a point of walking round the bus so that they were seen by everyone.

When the Royals arrived home, Philip was forbidden to appear among the welcoming party, for his presence would have sent an immediate signal to the public. Still living on his naval officer's pay, he had been saving up for an engagement ring, but in the event his mother provided the necessary jewels from family sources, including her own ring. The result was an arrangement with a solitaire diamond that had five smaller diamonds each side, set in platinum. The princess was given this at the beginning of July and wore it from then on. The wedding ring itself would not prove a financial setback, for the people of Wales donated one made from Welsh gold. The date was set for 20 November 1947. The *actual* engagement had been long – over a year – but the official one was to be short.

'Philip of Greece' had now become Lt Philip Mountbatten. His uncle's desire to see the family name linked with that of a reigning dynasty had very nearly been fulfilled.

It was felt by both the Palace and the Labour Government that the wedding should take place at St George's Chapel, Windsor. The country was still in a process of painful economic and material recovery from the war, and a low-key ceremony was considered in keeping with the times. As arrangements began to be discussed in the press, however, it quickly became clear that Parliament and the Royal Family had misread the national mood. After years of drabness and hardship the public longed to have spectacle again, and they wanted the bands and bunting they had not seen since the Coronation a decade before. The chapel, set in the Lower Ward of Windsor Castle and some 20 miles from London, was far too inaccessible and much too small for the crowds that wanted to join in the celebrations. These were quickly re-planned for Westminster Abbey. Expectations built up to such an extent that the wedding became a major state occasion. The Palace had to ask the Ministry of Food for extra rations to feed the foreign guests who would be coming.

There was a palpable yearning for splendour. This was to be the first time since 1939 that the coaches and colourful ceremonial uniforms – so vital a part of Britain's life and self-image – had been seen. It was more than a wish for something to look at, however. The bride and groom were both attractive, wholesome and personable. They featured heavily in the illustrated press, and something of a cult built around them. She was the nation's daughter. He looked like a film star, and the public had now accepted him. Moreover, they knew she had set her heart on him and had won him in spite of widespread disapproval (not least their own). This was a fairy tale that promised a happy ending. There was a rising tide of goodwill and popularity and expectation.

For her dress, Princess Elizabeth was granted a hundred additional clothing coupons, while each of her bridesmaids had 23. Norman Hartnell, who had already once outfitted her for a wedding (when she was bridesmaid to the Kents), produced

12 designs from which she could choose. She selected a pearl-white satin dress with a 15-foot train that fastened to the shoulders. It was embroidered with drop-pearls, seed-pearls and crystals, and had appliquéd orange-blossoms and star-flowers.

She wanted the music at her wedding to be memorable, and put much effort into this. The Abbey organist sent suggestions, and some were accepted, but her own memory provided other possibilities. She did not have a well-known bridal march, but opted for a piece by Parry from Aristophanes' *The Birds*. She requested 'Praise My Soul the King of Heaven', her favourite hymn, and 'The Lord's My Shepherd' in its Crimmond setting. For this, she favoured a descant that she had once heard in Scotland. No copy could be found anywhere but she sang it and Doctor McKie, the organist, wrote it down. It was eventually traced to a composer in Stirling who had written it for an Edinburgh girls' school.

There were to be 2,000 guests. Although a number of these were official, a surprising percentage were not and – apart from relations (Philip's sisters were not asked, because they were all married to Germans and feelings were still raw so soon after the war) many were there through appreciation of mundane services rendered. Their names had been found in letters, lists, diaries, or acquired by word of mouth. They included the stationmaster from Wolferton, the stop for Sandringham, the schoolmistress from Birkhall, the riding-instructors from Elizabeth's childhood, the young women who had made her wedding dress, and an American lady who had sent parcels to Philip throughout the war.

The event was to have film coverage, or rather cameras were to be positioned *outside* the Abbey. The service itself would be broadcast, but there was disquiet among some clergymen that it might be listened to by people drinking in public houses!

Presents poured in from all over the world. The Royal Family could not accept gifts other than from personal friends, and normal procedure would be to return them with a letter of thanks. The King, however, was so touched by his people's generosity that it was decided to keep them. They were put on display at St James's Palace and the public queued in droves to inspect them. At the suggestion of the Princess, a reception was also held for the donors. In total, 1,347 gifts were received – half the number that would be offered to her eldest son some 34 years later – and 20 of them came from Queen Mary alone. Some gifts have been in storage ever since. The largesse included a refrigerator, Purdey shotguns, and a Rolls-Royce that was a present from the RAF, as well as over a hundred pairs of nylon stockings – still a considerable luxury at the time – and numerous ration coupons. Some things could not be exhibited: the racehorse given by the Aga Khan and wittily named Astrakhan by Elizabeth, or the lodge presented by the government of Kenya.

Philip was also busy with preparations. He went, unobtrusively, to Lambeth Palace where in a brief ceremony conducted by the Archbishop of Canterbury he converted from Greek orthodoxy to the Church of England. He was also spoken to quietly, but extremely firmly, by one or two of his elders. Churchill, no longer premier but still wielding immense prestige, ensured that he realised the importance of the step he was taking. The King spoke to him in the way any future father-in-law is likely to do. In this case, he laid stress on Philip's tendency to flirt, and on his reckless driving. Interestingly, this latter gave the Princess an experience in common with many girls of her age. Her young man drove with impatient abandon. He had once put his sports car in a ditch and on another occasion, when with Elizabeth, had a contretemps with a taxi. She had wailed that this was not his fault but that her parents would not believe it. The King's concern was understandable. While every parent would worry about his daughter ending up in an accident, the implications in this case were very serious indeed.

The groom had lost his Greek citizenship, and his title, when naturalised. He was now simply Lieutenant Philip

Mountbatten, RN. Shortly before the wedding, however, the King made him Duke of Edinburgh – a title last used by one of Queen Victoria's sons – and he was installed as a Knight of the Garter. His fiancée had herself received the Garter a week earlier. Her father had been determined that she should precede her husband in membership, since she would in due course become head of the Order.

The evening before the wedding he had a bachelor party at the Dorchester hosted by his uncle. He stayed the night at Kensington Palace and the next day left for the Abbey with the best man, David Milford Haven. If he suffered any pre-wedding jitters, he did not let them show. Nor did he have a cigarette, as he might normally have done. He had been a smoker, but had now promised his wife-to-be that he would give up as a wedding present, and as far as is known he never touched another one.

There was a near mishap for the bride. When dressing at Buckingham Palace on the morning, she could not find the pearl necklace – a present – that she intended to wear. It transpired that it was still at St James's Palace where it was on display. Her Private Secretary, John Colville, had to be sent at once to fetch it. He arrived with no written authorisation, and was not known to the staff guarding the collection. Using all the charm and persuasiveness at his command, he managed to retrieve the necklace and get it to the Princess just in time.

The Archbishop of Canterbury, who officiated, stated in his address that the service 'is in all its essentials the same as it would be for any cottager who might be married this afternoon in some small country church', and that is how it was seen by many. The Royal Family, as maintained by George VI, was the middle class writ large. This was a family event on a national scale.

The bride showed impeccable poise. Her father later wrote of escorting her to the altar: 'You were so calm and composed during the Service & said your words with such conviction, that I knew everything was all right.' Elizabeth, of course, already knew more than most about solemn public declarations.

When the service ended, the guests returned to Buckingham Palace for the wedding breakfast. It comprised four courses, one of which was partridge from the Sandringham estate.

The couple went to Broadlands, the Hampshire country house of Lord Mountbatten, for the first days of their honeymoon (as Charles and Diana would later do). Travelling by carriage down Whitehall through the crowds to Waterloo Station – in an open carriage to allow people a good view, despite the bitter cold – there was sudden movement beneath the rug on their knees, and there appeared the head of Susan, the Princess's pet corgi. She had been smuggled along.

Such was the King's devotion to his daughter that she received a letter from him while at Broadlands and, when travelling through London to Scotland a few days later, she visited him at the Palace. While subsequent generations of royals have, on their honeymoons, been able to use *Britannia*, the Princess and the Duke went to Balmoral. However much their wedding had lifted the spirits of a country in the throes of austerity, their honeymoon was surely appropriate to the gloom of that time. November is arguably the dreariest month in the British calendar and, set between the foliage of autumn and the snows of Christmas, even a place so loved by the Princess might have seemed uninspiring.

This was the beginning of a marriage that has been extremely happy – a marriage of sympathetic companionship and mutual support in circumstances that would break most relationships. It was to cost Philip the naval career that he loved and was good at. Although he had the opportunity for a few years to live a normal life, he had to give it up, first gradually and then with awful suddenness, when his wife became Queen. He is a practical man, devoid of introspection, and that was just what the situation would need. He was to prove, in any case, equally successful in his new role. Not for nothing would Her Majesty describe him, decades later, as 'my rock'.

Despite their mutual devotion they were never to be demonstrative in public. Unlike American presidents, or British prime ministers before the advent of Blair, they would never hold hands, put their arms around each other, or be seen to kiss affectionately. That is their way, and it adds greatly to their dignity. A few years after their marriage Michael Parker, the Duke's Equerry, attempted to coax from him some spontaneity with regard to his wife, but in vain. Philip may not have had the Princess's sense of quiet reticence, but he has never believed in being emotional in public. As a naval officer he would have had views about appropriate – and inappropriate – behaviour while on duty. Elizabeth, too, has regarded herself as bound by the dignity of her position. Her parents, despite overwhelming mutual devotion, had never been given to such display. Royals believed that affection was a matter that could wait until they were out of sight.

Returning to London the young couple, in common with many people of their age in a country beset by a serious housing-shortage, moved in with their parents. They occupied the same suite of rooms at Buckingham Palace that the Princess had lived in when single and, by royal standards, this meant that they were somewhat cramped. They were supposed to reside at Clarence House in the Mall, one of several royal residences in the neighbourhood, but the building was so dilapidated that it required lengthy renovation, and brought public criticism for the £55,000 cost of this. There were so many work stoppages by the labourers involved that the King personally ordered them to 'stop taking so damned many tea-breaks'. Whether they followed this instruction is not known, but the house was still not ready when the couple began their family.

They did not move into Clarence House until the summer of 1949. They took great pleasure in planning the decor and installing the furniture and, like most young couples, they enjoyed the feeling that they had a home of their own. There was noisy public criticism regarding the lavishness of the interiors, which involved panelling in exotic woods, but in fact virtually all of these had been given by dominion governments or municipalities. The Duke's study, fitted with Canadian maple, was a wedding present. The Princess's bedroom was a gift from Glasgow.

The King had given them a country house at which to spend weekends. It was Sunningdale Park (a rebuilt version of this was to be bestowed on Prince Andrew at his wedding), near Windsor. Before they could occupy it, however, the house was destroyed by fire – perhaps the result of squatters. A replacement had quickly to be found and this was Windlesham Moor, a lavishly appointed house set in 50 acres of landscaped grounds not far from Ascot. It was described by the Princess's mother as 'more palatial than a palace' and was rented rather than bought. It was so big that its occupants could easily have got lost in either the house or the grounds. While it promised them all the privacy they could hope for, it was ironic that Elizabeth faced the prospect of spending time there alone. Her husband, still a serving naval officer, was soon to be posted overseas.

In the meantime, their first child was born. 'It's a boy!' announced the policeman on duty in the Palace forecourt, on 14 November 1948, to the crowd that had waited hours for news. Charles Philip Arthur George was born inside and, like his mother, by Caesarean section. Many people both within and without the family had expected a girl, given the preponderance of female children on both sides (Philip had four older sisters) and the public was delighted that the question of succession had been settled at once – had it been a girl, they might have had to wait years to see if a brother would follow. The Princess was an indulgent mother and she had, at that stage in her life, time to devote to her son. They would soon be separated.

Charles's birth was the first occasion on which such an event had taken place without the presence of the Home Secretary, a tradition that went back to 1688. The latest arrival was 82 years younger than the family's oldest member, and Queen Mary thus became a great-grandmother at a time when this was still unusual. Yet while the dowager queen still showed indomitable fitness, her son the King was failing. In 1949 he was only just well enough to appear at his birthday parade, and even then he was not mounted but in a carriage. He had been diagnosed with something called Buerger's disease, a condition that affects the arteries, and he also had bronchial carcinoma. There was considerable anxiety about his long-term, as well as short-term, health.

Philip had been working at the Admiralty and then at the Naval Staff College at Greenwich, appointments that kept him usefully within London. Indeed when at the Admiralty he lived no more than 10 minutes' walk from his desk and – amazingly, in view of the security that is necessary now – he travelled there alone and on foot. He could be seen leaving the Palace at half-past eight in the mornings to walk down the Mall, and the Princess could sometimes be glimpsed in late afternoon, looking out for his return from an upstairs window. He needed experience at sea, however, for career progress, and in 1949 he was sent to Malta to join the Mediterranean Fleet. His uncle, Lord Mountbatten, was there as commander of a cruiser squadron. The King was not happy about this posting for he knew Elizabeth would want to go too, and allowed her only on condition that she made regular returns to Britain. This was not merely a matter of sentiment – he was as reluctant as ever to part with her – but of duty. He needed his daughter to be able to deputise for him. His health had not recovered from the war (a chain-smoker, he was found to have lung cancer) but she was told only after Charles's birth how frail it was – and he was finding it harder to meet the physical demands of his role. On occasions that required the physical stamina to sit or stand for long periods, he was increasingly unable to cope. His daughter also had duties of her own. In the months and years after her wedding, she and Philip made tours of the United Kingdom so that her future peoples could see her, and her husband, at close quarters.

Nevertheless Elizabeth joined her husband. Charles stayed in London, and was looked after by his grandparents. The climate was considered unsuitable for a child of his years, and her own sense of duty dictated that she be with Philip. She had, after all, been left at home by her own parents at about the same age, and she was not going away for more than months at a time. She arrived in Valetta with 40 cases of clothing, her car and a polo pony. This game was a passion among servicemen on the island and Philip, who had already proved an extremely sound cricketer, was in the process of learning it.

The couple remained in Malta, on and off, between 1949 and 1951. Despite interruptions and increasing worry over the King's health, it was to be a golden interlude in their lives, a period upon which they would look back with warm nostalgia. As well as the pleasure of serving at sea, Philip was able to feel relatively free from the strait-jacket of Court life, and Elizabeth could experience the nearest thing she would ever know to normal existence. Their surroundings were glorious and the pace of life agreeably slow, with much time given to polo and other sporting events. Philip was given his own ship, HMS *Magpie*. Command was the ambition of every naval officer, and he lost no time in putting on the vessel and its crew the stamp of his personality. Like his uncle he had a passion for winning trophies, showing off and being the best at everything. He drove his men in competition but took part himself, pulling an oar in the races that won *Magpie* the title Cock of the Flotilla.

'The Med' was not a Cold War flashpoint and Britain's problems in the region – Suez and Cyprus – were several years off. The Navy could devote time to fostering international goodwill, and its royal officer and his wife were ideal for this. *Magpie* made a number of leisurely official visits to Heads of State in the region. Between calls there were cocktail parties, receptions, picnics and swimming. Small wonder that *Magpie* was known in the Navy as 'Edinburgh's private yacht'. This would, in normal circumstances, have been the first of many commands in a career alternating between sea and shore duty. Philip was not to know that it would be the height of his active service, and the only vessel he ever commanded.

Elizabeth was in some respects able to live as an officer's wife, but this must not be overstated. She was scarcely more a 'normal' wife than she had been a normal officer in the ATS. As with so many things, she could experience it only partially, fleetingly, under strictly controlled and largely artificial conditions. Although she enjoyed expeditions to shops and markets and the hairdresser, to dances and swimming-parties and even to sit in the back row of the cinema, she was not in any sense anonymous. She was not in a foreign country – Malta was, at the time, as British as any other colony – and she was thus the daughter of the ruler. She was living not in Married Quarters but, initially at least, in the villa of her husband's uncle. Unlike other wives she had a dresser and a footman, was followed everywhere by a detective, and had always to be addressed as 'Ma'am'. She carried out some low-key official duties, visiting servicemens' clubs or giving out trophies. She also had to commute home on a regular basis. She was required to deputise for the King in receiving visits from the French President and the kings of Denmark and Norway. She travelled by air between Britain and the Mediterranean to save time.

She was, in fact, never able to settle down in Malta. In the midst of Philip's posting – on 15 August 1950 – her second child Princess Anne was born, in England. The Princess was therefore at home for several months, and her husband for several weeks. When she eventually rejoined him, there were pointed comments in the press about her neglect of her children.

Philip, despite his commitments, was inevitably drawn into public life too. The couple had already made an official visit to Paris, and now they were asked to undertake a tour of Canada and the USA in October 1951. The King and Queen had intended going – this would have been their first postwar visit to North America – but had abruptly had to cancel when the King's health once again took a turn for the worse. There was now not time for the young couple to make the journey by sea, and Philip suggested they fly instead. This was a novel suggestion, characteristic of his practicality and impatience with restrictive traditional practice. Transatlantic flight was lengthy and uncomfortable (it included a refuelling stop) and fears for the safety of the Royal Family meant that the Prime Minister had to give permission for the flight. He was persuaded, and they became the first royals to make this journey. Such was the worry about the King's health that Elizabeth's Private Secretary carried with him a sealed envelope to be opened in the event of his death. It contained an address to both houses of Parliament.

They spent a month in Canada and the USA. They had planned for this journey with a thoroughness that was to become habitual, devoting long hours to reading and discussion, building a detailed knowledge of even the smallest places they would visit. As an attractive young couple who had not been seen before by the people of the Dominion they were popular, though Philip was to cause some offence by referring to Canada, in a speech, as 'a good investment'. He was pictured square-dancing in western clothes while she wore a print skirt (these had had to be swiftly bought by their staff on the day of the dance. Philip's jeans were later found to have the price tag still on them), which was a thing no royals had previously done. They passed on to the USA where they stayed at Blair House (the White House was being renovated) as guests of the Trumans. The President was very taken with them, sending the King a message afterwards that: 'They went to the hearts of all the citizens. As one father to another,' he went on, 'you can be very proud.' Despite the goodwill they generated, Philip's irascibility was in evidence. Irritated by the noise of Secret Service agents patrolling the corridors at night, he said to their chief: 'Tell me, do you employ professional door-slammers in this building?'

Their visit was seen by the King as such a triumph that he made both of them Privy Councillors when they got home. Having proved themselves both officially and personally, they were asked by the Government to perform the same duty the following year. This time it would be a much longer tour, lasting six months in all, to Australia and New Zealand, visiting Kenya and Ceylon on the way. Once again the King and Queen had intended to make the journey themselves, but he had had to undergo a lung operation, and travel was out of the question. Philip was given indefinite leave from the Navy. His full-time job – at least until his father-in-law's health improved – was to support his wife in her official duties.

On 31 January 1952 they departed from Britain by air and the King, Queen and Margaret saw them off. Although pictures of this event show the King looking stooped and unwell, his family were optimistic. His operation had been successful, and the auguries were good. 'Look out for yourselves,' were his parting words to his daughter. She would, once again, be avoiding a bleak English winter in the line of duty. The tour would be extremely taxing, so it was arranged that in Kenya she and Philip would have, after a few days of official functions, a rest amid the idyllic scenery of the highlands – though this was marred at the time by the vicious and destructive Mau Mau rebellion.

They stayed at Saguna Lodge, their wedding present from the colony, and on 5 February 1952 they arrived at the Treetops Hotel. Built into a giant wild fig tree, the structure was not a conventional hotel but a series of private rooms and a viewing platform in the branches above a watering-hole. This had been designed to allow guests to watch animals coming at dusk to drink. The young couple were very excited by the prospect. The Princess, wearing jeans, used her cine camera to great effect. Darkness fell. She, her husband and her staff retired to sleep and during the night – no one knows exactly when – she became queen.

Far away, at Sandringham, the Royal family also retired to bed. The King had spent a highly enjoyable day shooting – it was the end of the season – with his keepers. He had joked with the Queen and Margaret during dinner, and had gone to his room in good spirits. By the following morning he had died, of thrombosis.

The news did not officially reach his daughter. The code-name for this event – planned, like everything to do with royalty, long in advance – was 'Hyde Park Corner'. The telegram did not get through because it is thought the operator mistook the contents for the address. The news was instead picked up by a journalist friend of Elizabeth's Private Secretary Martin Charteris, passed by him to the Duke's Equerry Michael Parker and thence to Philip and to Elizabeth. She was allowed some privacy, of course, to absorb the shock. She walked a little way, deep in talk with her husband. When she appeared, to speak to her staff, she had mastered whatever emotions had immediately affected her, and was as self-contained and resolute as they had expected. The moment she had awaited, imagined – perhaps dreaded – had come. She might have said, as did Churchill when he became Prime Minister in 1940: 'I felt ... as if all my past life had been but a preparation for this hour and for this trial.' Since she was now sovereign, the world must know at once what her name was to be, and which of her christened names she would choose: Queen Elizabeth, Queen Alexandra or Queen Mary. Might her preference be in tribute to her mother, grandmother or great-grandmother? She had had many years in which to think about this but her reply, when asked by Charteris how she would be known, was characteristically brisk: 'My own name, of course, what else?'

The first thing the new Queen said to her assembled staff was typical of the young woman who had been brought up to consider others before herself: 'I am so sorry that it means we've got to go back to England and it's upsetting everybody's plans.'

Also characteristic was her concern for her mother and sister. She had a new role to assume and a wealth of things to do that would occupy her mind and energies. They would have nothing but a sense of devastation.

Stories of the King's death sometimes suggest that his daughter was interrupted by the news in the midst of a tranquil holiday. In fact, the royal party had been due to leave within hours for Mombassa where the SS *Gothic* – there was no royal yacht at the time – was waiting to take them to Ceylon. Their luggage was already aboard, including Elizabeth's mourning clothes.

She flew home by the most direct route, across North Africa. During a brief stopover, instructions were telegraphed to London. She would be greeted by the Prime Minister and the Cabinet, and would be seen by the world's press the moment she emerged from the aircraft. She could not be wearing anything but black.

She came home not six months, but six days, after she had left. The plane bumped onto the runway but stopped some distance from where the official delegation waited. A car raced across the tarmac and stopped under the fuselage. Luggage was heaved aboard. The aircraft taxied with deliberate slowness, going no faster than walking pace while the Queen swiftly dressed in mourning. She came down the steps alone in her black dress and hat, her subjects' first glimpse of their new sovereign. When the Prime Minister, Churchill, offered sympathy she remarked: 'A tragic homecoming, but a smooth flight.'

Driven to St James's Palace, she made an accession speech that was brief and poignant: 'My heart is too full for me to say more to you today than that I shall always work as my father did.' Shortly afterwards she went on to Sandringham where he lay in state in the church, watched over by estate workers. She curtsied to his coffin – the last time she would ever make such a gesture.

# YOUNG QUEEN, 1952–1960

'Charming little creature!
I only hope they don't work her too hard.'

For the second time in her life, Elizabeth had to move to
Buckingham Palace from a home she loved. This time she gave
up Clarence House more or less at the moment she and Philip
had finished turning it into a family home. So much trouble
had gone into its renovation, so much of their own time and
enthusiasm had been expended on the choosing of furniture,
pictures and colour schemes, that it was heartbreaking to leave
it. The senior Queen Elizabeth, for whom the Palace was associated with her husband, was as reluctant to move from her
home as the junior one was to take her place. Both asked the
Prime Minister if they could not stay where they were. Might
the new sovereign not use the Palace as her office and live, as it
were, next door? Churchill would not hear of it. Buckingham
Palace was not simply a home. It was a symbol of the nation
and the Empire, and it was unthinkable that a reigning monarch
should reside anywhere else. The elder Queen, who was to
share Clarence House with Princess Margaret, proved rather

stubborn. To gain her consent the Prime Minister had to agree that a fireplace – a gift from the King – could be dismantled and brought with her.

Her daughter had more pressing matters to consider. Despite the training she had had, she had much to learn about the day-to-day work of being monarch. She was later to recall that, thrust into her position: 'It was all very sudden, kind of taking on and making the best job you can . . . a question of just maturing into what you're doing and accepting that here you are and it's your fate.' Nevertheless she proved extremely adept at administration and paperwork. She was as conscientious as the late King, but could read the papers in her dispatch boxes at twice the speed, while remembering most of their contents. She was brisk, but thorough. Her questions to officials were penetrating and her opinions perceptive.

At least her Coronation was not one of her principal worries. It was decided that it would take place in June 1953 – 16 months after her accession – and this allowed time for the preparations to be organised and carried out without haste, as well as for the manufacture and marketing of souvenirs. As early as the previous November the route was timed and tested. In December the Abbey was closed for a period of nine months and handed over to the Ministry of Works, which began the task of transforming it for the ceremony. All the chairs were removed, and the great church filled with planks and scaffolding (there was even a small set of railway tracks for moving heavy objects). Huge electric lights were rigged above the nave. Rows of benches were constructed, as steeply raked as the seats in a theatre, and once complete were crowded with soldiers to test their strength. Balconies were decorated with blue-and-gold hangings. In the crossing, which for crownings is known as the Theatre, the Coronation chair was set. Behind it was the dais, five steps high (so that the sovereign could be clearly seen) and copied from a medieval original, on which she would sit to receive the homage of her noblemen.

The Duke of Norfolk, who as Earl Marshal was hereditary master of ceremonies, presided over rehearsals that were
compulsory for all the principals involved except the Queen
(she was represented by his wife). He was aware that some
previous coronations, such as Victoria's, had been disorgan-
ised to the point of farce, and was determined that there would
be no mistakes. Practice went on every day of the week.

At the Palace, too, rehearsals were lengthy and serious. The
Queen listened, over and over, to records made of her father's
Coronation ceremony, memorising the order of prayers and
hymns and movements, supplementing her own memories of
the event.

Draped in sheets that enabled her to accustom to carrying a
long train, she processed around the White Drawing Room –
chosen because it was much the same size as the crossing in the
Abbey – to determine how slowly she should walk and how
many paces it would take to get from place to place. In the
Picture Gallery chairs were arranged into an approximation
of the state coach so that she, with her train, could practise
getting in and out. The train was to be carried by six maids-
of-honour, all the daughters of peers. They had been chosen
by the Earl Marshal and were perhaps somewhat baffled, until
they met. It then became obvious that they had been carefully
selected for height with two tall, two medium and two shorter
girls.

Beyond the Palace railings, the public was also gearing up for
what was to be – even more than her wedding and the Festival
of Britain – the greatest national celebration of recent times.
This would be the fourth coronation of the 20th century (there
had been three in the 19th) but it was an event rare enough to
be savoured, and something that would naturally be remembered for the whole of their lives by those who were there. This
fact was not lost on manufacturers, who began using images
of the Queen to decorate all manner of commercial products.
No doubt the Coronation biscuit-barrels were expected to be

cherished by posterity, but more ephemeral packaging used her likeness too. The rate of exposure increased as June came nearer, and caused a certain amount of visual fatigue. 'Not that I've anything against the Queen,' one woman lamented, 'I'm just sick of seeing her face on everything from tinned peas upwards.'

One thing threatened to spoil the event. The new Queen's grandmother was in rapidly failing health and her death, weeks or even days before the ceremony, would oblige the court to go into mourning. The older Queen had suffered several major blows since the death of her husband in 1936: the Abdication, the war, the loss of the Indian Empire (for which she held Mountbatten, the last Viceroy, personally responsible) and the death of her son, the King, at the age of only 56. The single thing she hoped to see was her granddaughter wearing the crown. When the date was set for June, it became a race against time, and the old lady lost. She would not allow her own situation to interfere with the sovereign's crowning, however, and insisted that court mourning should not be imposed if she died beforehand. She did, on 24 March – exactly 70 days before the event. It is believed that before this Elizabeth visited her – and put on the crown.

The immense respect that the new Queen's parents had earned throughout the war meant that the Royal Family could bank on a huge amount of public goodwill. Elizabeth herself was deeply popular, still young and strikingly beautiful, and now with a family of her own. Press and people were at a pitch of uncritical admiration that would last a few further years before the age of debunking and levelling began.

Publishers filled the bookshops and news-stands with material on the sovereign, her family and her homes and – to set it all in context – the history of coronations, of the offices of state, of the Crown Jewels and of the Abbey itself. Of all national occasions, none is as grand as a coronation. Other events – openings of Parliament, jubilees, even royal weddings and funerals – do not assemble all the colourful office-holders, feature the same wealth of bands and flags, or deploy the full majesty of British tradition to the same extent. The lesser occasions are separate parts, this is the whole – the oldest, the biggest, the most elaborate royal ceremony, a fusion of sacred and secular, ancient and modern, civilian and military. Because India had become independent Elizabeth could not become an Empress, but there was compensation in that she would inherit no less than 13 thrones as queen, by invitation, of Canada, Australia, New Zealand and other nations and territories. Editorials lectured on the significance of what was to occur, described some of the 38 previous coronations in the Abbey, and dispensed advice on vantage-points as well as offering tips on how to survive the waiting and the weather.

For those who could not endure a night on cold paving stones – or could not get to London in the first place – there was considerable joy in the news that the ceremony would be televised. The body responsible for planning the event was the Coronation Committee, and this had announced that there would be no cameras in the Abbey. The result was such an outcry that the issue had to be reconsidered. The decision was not taken lightly. The Government, the Church and the Queen were all opposed, and it was intended that only a radio broadcast be allowed. It was, after all, not a tourist spectacle but a religious service, and it was thought that the presence of cameras and film-crews among the costumed dignitaries would distract as well as detract from the solemnity of the occasion. Not only that, but it would be extremely lengthy. The service would last seven hours and 15 minutes. Could an audience, even seated comfortably at home, endure such a marathon? The final decision was left to the Queen but, since the others involved had come round to the idea, she agreed. This meant that make-up would have to be applied to those on whom the cameras focused.

Not all of the proceedings were to be seen. The receiving of communion by the sovereign was deemed too private and too sacred a thing to broadcast but the more 'public' parts of the event – the recognition, the oath, the anointing, the investiture and the homage – would be witnessed by a worldwide audience. It was the Queen who decided that the route followed by her carriage through London should be significantly lengthened, so that more people would have the chance to see her. She also asked that places along the way be especially allocated to schoolchildren.

The State Coach was refurbished and modernised, its iron tyres replaced with rubber for smoother travel, and the lighting inside it improved to make the occupants more clearly visible. It was also, unbeknown to the crowds, fitted inside with a cumbersome wireless so that the Queen and her husband could hear the BBC commentary as they travelled to the Abbey.

In the days before 2 June, London filled with both visitors and participants. The latter included some 15,000 troops who would line the streets or march in the procession. Their tents filled the parks, which were made off-limits to civilians.

The day itself mocked any notion of 'Queen's weather' – the sunshine that is supposed to accompany royal occasions. It was misty, cold and very wet although the spectators, sleepless and huddled along the roadsides, succeeded in enjoying it regardless. The Queen began it as she had begun her father's Coronation day – by looking out at the early morning crowds from an upstairs window of the Palace. They still had several hours to wait but at half-past ten the State Coach, its gold paintwork contrasting with the dismal grey sky, emerged from the Palace gates. The pent-up enthusiasm of the thousands who lined the Mall was released in a tidal wave of cheering. Preceded by the Sovereign's Escort of Household Cavalry, accompanied on horseback and afoot by a splendidly uniformed entourage, the Queen and her consort moved down the Mall at walking pace (the coach is too heavy to travel any faster). Soldiers presented arms, the crowds yelled, applauded, waved flags. The coach turned right down Whitehall and traversed Parliament Square to arrive at the Abbey's West Door, which was obscured by a decorative temporary annexe. The youth and beauty of the sovereign, as well as her enthusiasm for her role, made a deep impression on those who saw her that day. 'Charming little creature!' enthused one of them, Lord Pethwick-Lawrence. 'I only hope they don't work her too hard.'

Waiting inside was a congregation of more than 8,000 people that included the prime ministers of the Commonwealth countries. In the streets were two million spectators. The service – all seven hours of it – was watched on three million televisions in Britain by up to 27 million viewers, four-fifths of the population. Many people bought the first television their family had owned in order to see the ceremony. Others landed themselves on friends and relatives to sit clustered in front of the screen, just as a generation earlier they had sat around the wireless to hear George VI crowned. Celebrations were held throughout the Commonwealth and the Empire and beyond. Within the community of British nations, cities were decorated with bunting and filled with marching troops and parading dignitaries. There was, in those days, no question of seeing the service live on television overseas, but it could be heard on radio and – in the days afterward – viewed as a full-scale film. Narrated by the actress Anna Neagle, this was to be watched in cinemas all over the globe. In the Irish Republic, which had severed its links with the Crown some years earlier, it was withdrawn from picture-houses after bomb threats by extremists, but it was viewed surreptitiously in church halls by largely Protestant audiences. It was an event that raised morale throughout the world, and even countries without any British connection became involved. Brazil, neither a former colony nor a member of the Commonwealth, made the sovereign a present. It was a necklace and a pair of earrings of diamonds and aquamarines, and it was no mere official gesture. It was a gift from the Brazilian people, not their government, and it had taken them a year to assemble the stones. They were later to add a matching bracelet – a most generous offering from a generous nation. The Queen would wear these jewels on her state visit to the country 15 years later.

For the hungry there had been good news. Rationing of eggs was ended and – to the delight of the youngest of Elizabeth's subjects – so was that of sweets. Everyone was allocated an additional pound of sugar to allow the making of cakes. The Coronation really seemed as if some magic wand had been waved and the world transported back – for just a few hours – to pre-war days.

The queen had arrived wearing an elaborately embroidered dress but she re-appeared, as custom dictated, in a 'linen shift' – effectively the plain, short-sleeved white shirt of a medieval peasant, in order to present an image of simplicity and humility. On top of this, as the ceremony went on, was placed her long, velvet-and-ermine robe (embroidered in gold, in frantic haste, by a team at the Royal School of Needlework) and then she was given the accoutrements of office: the orb, the sceptre and the amulets (a gift from the Commonwealth). The holy oil with which she was to be anointed was unavailable, having been lost in wartime bombing, and a similar concoction had had to be mixed at Savory and Moore, the perfumers in Bond Street. Last came the St Edward's Crown itself, a replacement dating from the Coronation of Charles II for the original that had disappeared at the time of Cromwell.

It weighed seven pounds – in addition to the 17 pounds of her robes. She was so heavily burdened that, after being crowned, she had to be lifted and steered gently to the dais by the Archbishop of Canterbury and others. It had been suggested that the crown be made lighter for her, but with her characteristic stoicism she had insisted that if her father had worn it so could she. To an extraordinary extent it symbolises the history of the nation and Empire. One of its stones – a sapphire – is reputed to have belonged to the Abbey's first builder, Edward the Confessor. Another was owned by Mary, Queen of Scots. Another – the Black Prince's Ruby – was actually worn by King Henry V at Agincourt and again by Richard III at Bosworth. A fourth was worn in exile by King James II. The crown even incorporates the pearl earrings of Elizabeth I. It was as if the sovereign were wearing on her head a summing-up of British history and national greatness, which of course she was.

Her husband, also in ermine-lined velvet robes but dressed as an Admiral of the Fleet, was the first secular figure to pay her homage. Her mother and sister were both present, watching from a gallery nearby. Her son, not yet five, was there too although he had not been considered old enough to watch the whole of the lengthy proceedings, and had been spirited in only for the most important phase. Her daughter, less than three, was altogether too young and had been left at home, where a children's party was going on.

The ceremony included a beautiful prayer that asked: 'The Lord give you faithful parliaments and quiet realms; sure defence against all enemies; fruitful lands and upright magistrates; leaders of integrity in learning and labour; a devout, learned and useful clergy; honest, peaceable and dutiful citizens.' Curious as it may seem from a later perspective, there was a widespread feeling in Britain that the start of this reign marked the beginning of a New Elizabethan Age, that the nation was on the cusp of an era to rival the Tudors. The phrase – mere journalistic hyperbole – was seen and heard everywhere, and sent many people in search of similarities and coincidences. It was viewed as significant not only that the two queens shared a name but that they had both come to the throne at the age of 25. A very distinct echo of the Elizabethan age of discovery – and a bright augury for the future – was heard with the news, released on the morning of the Coronation, that Everest had been climbed by an expedition led by one of her subjects (a New Zealander) and that the Union Flag had been planted on the summit.

For the banquet that followed the ceremony Prue Leith, the doyenne of English cooks, devised a dish that she called Coronation Chicken. The chicken was covered in a creamy mayonnaise sauce with mild curry powder and was a rich gold in colour. In later versions it also had sultanas and sliced almonds. It has been ever since a much-loved sandwich filling and is ubiquitous on supermarket shelves all over the United Kingdom. Despite the perishable nature of its ingredients it has proved the most enduring as well as the most popular Coronation souvenir.

The whole event was extensively reported in newspapers all over the world. The tone – with the predictable exception of the left-wing press and Communist countries – was indulgent, fulsome and awestruck. Nowhere outside the Arabian Nights was there such splendour. A feast of colour and pageantry, ancient ritual and popular celebration, all carried out with characteristic understatement and perfect timing. The fact that the new sovereign was a demure and beautiful young woman added immensely to the charm of the event, as it had when Victoria was crowned 115 years earlier. It was also a moment of national affirmation for, although Elizabeth's country had survived the war, its Empire was fast unravelling. Britain was no longer rich enough to belong to the Great Powers Club. Before the conflict had even ended, the US dollar had ousted sterling as the world's most important currency, and America and Russia had simply elbowed Britain aside and gone on to dominate the world between them. The British people needed the rhetoric of the New Elizabethan Age to bolster a confidence that was otherwise seeping away. With the Coronation the United Kingdom was able, for a few hours or days, to lead the world in *something*, to compel international attention and respect, to foster envy in others. It emphasised all the things that money could not buy nor sudden poverty negate – breeding, heritage, long-developed self-assurance that could so easily shade into a smug belief that 'no one can do these things like we do'. It was what the Festival of Britain two years earlier was supposed to have been – a signal that Britain had recovered from the war and was once again a happy nation, its technology and culture leading it back to prosperity.

It might have come as a pleasant surprise, to those who regretted Britain's ousting from pre-eminence by America, to learn that at least 40,000 Americans came to London for the Coronation and that berths aboard the Atlantic liners were all-but-impossible to obtain. In addition to these, an estimated 55 million – almost a third of the population – watched the ceremony on television in the USA. It was not possible to show it live, but the Royal Air Force flew over the BBC tapes so that it could be screened within hours. Among transatlantic guests at the ceremony were George Marshall and Omar Bradley, towering figures in the recent war, and Jacqueline Bouvier who, as Mrs John F. Kennedy (she married him that year), would go on to be seen as her own country's equivalent of royalty. More unusually there was George Davis, a native of New Hampshire, who owed his invitation to a casual meeting with the Queen two years earlier, when he was standing outside Clarence House and Prince Charles ran over to show him a picture book; part of royalty's fairy-tale appeal is the way in which ordinary people can be swept up in its doings through chance.

Once the Coronation was over, the next event was a tour of the Commonwealth. This was to be a massive undertaking. It would last six months, from 25 November 1953 to 15 May 1954 – the Queen's children would not see their parents for all that time – and would cover a total of 43,618 miles. Some countries, such as Australia and New Zealand, had not been visited since before the war. With smaller territories it could not be assumed, given her busy schedule, that the Queen would have time to go there again during her reign. This might be their only glimpse of her.

The journey took in the West Indies, Australia, New Zealand, and parts of Asia and Africa. In the course of this it is estimated that she listened to 276 speeches and 508 renditions of 'God Save the Queen'. Although she set off aboard the SS *Gothic* she would travel, at least some of the distance (the homeward stretch from Malta), in the Royal Yacht. This vessel had been planned and begun before King George's death, but had been completed after Elizabeth's accession, and was launched by her. She had decided to discontinue the name *Victoria and Albert* (there had been three of these), ignored suggestions that *The Elizabeth* would be appropriate, and chose *Britannia*. At 412 feet in length and weighing 5,862 tons, the yacht was the size of a small warship and as luxurious as a country house – on which, in fact, the interiors were modelled. The yacht had a State Dining Room that could seat 56 (and doubled as a cinema), as well as a drawing room, separate sitting rooms for the Queen and the Duke, accommodation for the Household, their staff and the crew, and a 'barracks' for the Marine band that accompanied them on official visits. This was a vessel worthy of the New Elizabethan Age, a leviathan that could cross the world's oceans and bring the refinement – and the magic – of Buckingham Palace to distant continents. It provided a perfect setting for the monarch when overseas, and enabled her to return hospitality in suitable style.

On her return, the Prime Minister came aboard *Britannia* off the Isle of Wight and accompanied the Queen to London. The sight of the Royal Yacht steaming up the Thames and beneath Tower Bridge, with the sovereign and the Premier on board, has become one of the most glorious images of her reign. Visible to the crowds on the banks as a tiny, waving figure, she gave no sign of fatigue despite having to remain in that position for over four hours.

At home, there was a simmering problem. Princess Margaret had been for some time involved in a relationship that was considered unsuitable. Group Captain Peter Townsend had been an Equerry of her father's. He was a Battle of Britain fighter pilot, and King George had wanted one of these men attached to his staff as a tribute to their courage. Townsend was a success with the family. He was charming, modest, efficient, and had a pleasant sense of humour. He fitted in so well that he rose from temporary Equerry to Deputy Master of the Household, a position for which, at 36, he was young. Margaret was 16 years his junior and had first met him when aged 13. Idolising her father, she perhaps found it natural to admire an older man, and her girlish affection matured into a serious regard. In the small world of the Court they could not have avoided each other, and he accompanied the family on its tour of South Africa. By the time of Elizabeth's Coronation they were deeply attached. What is surprising is that her family remained unaware of this burgeoning romance until Margaret announced her wish to marry him. They had not seen it as unusual that she spent long periods of time with him, often alone.

With his war record, his easy charm, integrity and familiarity with the ways of the Court, Townsend would have made a highly successful consort. Even in the 1950s there might have been no strenuous objection to the Queen's sister marrying this presentable commoner, but for the fact that Townsend was divorced. He was the wronged party, and his marriage had been a hasty wartime one, but this made no difference. The Anglican Church, of which the Queen was Head, could not sanction such a high-profile union involving a divorcee. It was also considered, within the Royal Household, that as a Court official he should not have had the presumption to allow this friendship to begin and to develop. Prince Philip disliked Townsend and had the ear of the Queen, who had the power to veto the marriage, for under the Royal Marriages Act she must approve all spouses. With such powerful disapproval and opposition, the relationship was not likely to flourish. The matter was kept from press and public but by a quirk of fate a journalist, Audrey Whiting, spotted Margaret, who was outside the Abbey following the Coronation, make some adjustment to – probably flicking off a speck of dust – the uniform of an RAF officer, who was soon identified. It was a gesture of such obvious intimacy that the game was up.

The press unearthed the whole story of their friendship. Margaret was a somewhat spoiled young woman who was used to wheedling until she got what she wanted. She had expected her mother and sister to side with her because they had both remained relatively passive when she had told them of the situation. She came to realise, however, that this was because both of them wished to avoid confrontation and were hoping that somehow the problem would solve itself. Townsend was transferred to Brussels as Air Attaché to get him out of the way. He remained there for two years, but this was not a distant exile and the press was able to speculate that the couple were still in contact. When he returned, public speculation was at fever pitch. Whatever the view of the Court, a good deal of public opinion supported Margaret's right to marry the man she loved, yet if she did so she would have to give up all the privileges of her rank. She would find herself living with a husband whose salary could not possibly keep her. Both parties discussed the future and decided that it was not viable for them to remain together. The Archbishop of Canterbury, on whom Margaret called at Lambeth Palace, was brusquely told he could put away all the arguments he had been marshalling to persuade her to reconsider. She had already done so. She issued a simple statement that read, in part: 'I have decided not to marry

Group Captain Townsend. Subject to my renouncing my rights of succession, it might have been possible for me to contract a civil marriage, but ... conscious of my duty to the Commonwealth, I have resolved to put these considerations before all others.' All her life, Margaret was attached to the privileges that went with being royal. Without them she would have been miserable, and this influenced her choice. Nevertheless her decision to put duty before her own wishes was an uncanny echo of the abdication crisis of 1936, although with the opposite outcome.

The Townsend affair was the beginning of the modern era in terms of Royalty and the media. The scandal surrounding Edward VIII had not been reported because the press had agreed to gag itself. George VI, Queen Elizabeth and Princess Elizabeth had given reporters nothing to feed upon. Now there was a story that enabled the public to look inside the private lives of the Windsors, to take sides, to criticise. Coming at a time when respect for all authority was declining, this showed that no institution could take for granted the goodwill of the public, or hope that its faults would not be analysed and commented upon. It represented a sea change in the attitude of a press that had deferred to the throne since the 1870s. Even though both parties in the relationship behaved honourably – their self-restraint and self-discipline in the face of a painful separation were deeply impressive – their private lives were seen as public property.

The Coronation had awakened a sense of pageantry as well as patriotism, and the Royal Family was able once again to provide a focus for this. The Queen attended Trooping the Colour dressed not – as she had been in the 1940s – in a dark blue uniform with a peaked cap, but in a magnificent scarlet cutaway coat in the pattern of the 18th century and faced with the buttons of whichever regiment was parading its colour that day. She wore a dark blue long skirt and a low, black hat of unique design on which the regiment's cap-badge and plume were displayed. She also wore the medals to which she was entitled through her wartime service, and it is easy to imagine how proud of these she would have been for, unlike the Order of the Garter that she also wore, she owed them not to her position but to having performed the same duties as thousands of other young women. She sat side-saddle, a thing she never did when riding for pleasure but which gave her an appropriate dignity. When going to and from this event along the Mall, she looked straight ahead and remained expressionless. Those among the watching crowds who came from more exuberant cultures often wondered why she did not smile or even acknowledge their presence, and may have interpreted her apparent aloofness as disdain. The answer was, of course, that she was a soldier on duty, attending a parade. Throughout the ceremony itself she sat stiffly to attention, unable to show the least sign of fatigue or – in the June heat – discomfort, and she saluted smartly. Everything about her had the customary sense of patient dedication to detail. One senior officer remarked gruffly that 'she's the only woman I know who can salute properly', but of course she would have trained as hard as any man on the parade ground.

Despite an affectionate marriage, the Queen and Prince Philip were often apart, especially as his own sphere of activity expanded. In 1956 he went, with his wife's blessing, on a voyage on *Britannia* that lasted four months. He had missed the active life of the Navy, and this was an opportunity to revive something valuable from his past. After opening the Melbourne Olympics he wandered the Southern Hemisphere, visiting a number of British territories that, because of their intense isolation, did not see Royalty from one reign to the next: the Falkland Islands, Tristan da Cuhna, St Helena. He travelled almost 40,000 miles. This meant, of course, that he was away from his growing children and missed Christmas with them. He was also absent throughout the Suez Crisis, when he could have been a steadying public presence. His

long maritime odyssey also fuelled rumours that his marriage
was in difficulties, though it was probably approved by the
Queen as compensation for his lost naval career and as a
break from Court ritual. His Equerry and general assistant,
Michael Parker, was to be sued for divorce on their return –
this news leaked and obliged him to resign his position before
the voyage even ended – and neither man was in a hurry to get
back. Philip finally saw the Queen again in Portugal, where
they were making a state visit together. It was known that he
had grown a beard at one point during the voyage, and when
he was reunited with his wife aboard an aircraft he found that
she, and her ladies-in-waiting, were all sporting false whiskers.
Her Majesty, in spite of this, does not like facial hair, and he
would have been unlikely to keep his beard.

Amid the stresses of her new role, she found enormous
pleasure in escaping to the world of the Turf. Since her wartime
encounters with this (in 1945 she began her regular annual
attendances at Ascot) she had been edging closer to serious
involvement, and in 1949 she had taken the first step. She and
her mother, who had a similar wish to dabble in racing, had
been persuaded to purchase between them a steeplechaser
called Monaveen. Although soundly recommended and
initially successful, Monaveen died during a race and, while
her mother remained devoted to steeplechasing, the Princess
decided to abandon 'the sticks' for flat racing. Only after the
death of the Queen Mother in 2002 would her daughter take
over her 'jumpers'.

She had introduced personal racing colours; scarlet and
with purple hoops on the sleeves, and a black cap. These were
given up when she succeeded because she then inherited the
Royal colours, which had first been adopted by the Prince
Regent: purple body with gold braid and scarlet sleeves. Black
cap with a gold fringe (Princess Anne would revive and use
the old colours when riding in a race in 1987). She began to
regularly attend race-meetings and, since her husband did not

share her enthusiasm, she was often in the company of Henry Herbert, Lord Porchester. 'Porchie' was to become her closest male friend. She had known him since they were both at Windsor during the war, and they had met at debutante parties. His knowledge of the Turf was an inspiration to her, and in 1969 she would appoint him her Racing Manager – a post he continued to hold even after he succeeded as seventh Earl of Caernarvon. They would speak on the phone very frequently – often daily – and his calls were put through immediately by the Palace switchboard. Another who shared her passion was Winston Churchill, her Prime Minister during the years of her reign. Himself a successful owner, he could talk knowledgeably with her about horses once more weighty matters had been dealt with at their weekly audiences.

Given a thoroughbred as a wedding present, she had begun what would become a lifelong career as breeder and owner. When this fascination had matured, the means to further it already existed, in the shape of the Royal Stud. Moved to Sandringham from its out-of-the-way setting at Hampton Court, this blossomed under the patronage of the new Queen. She had begun to take a close interest in horse breeding, for she found that this was a field that favoured her strengths. A lifetime's experience in the saddle, as well as long years of listening to stable-talk among experts, had given her an impressive ability to judge a horse's temperament and to assess its potential. Although she would never ride in a race herself she began, in 1954, a tradition during Ascot Week of visiting the course on horseback early in the mornings to ride round it, accompanied by some of those who stayed with her at Windsor for the event. She could therefore sometimes add to her knowledge of horses a personal experience of the track. Although she has horses trained and bred – she usually has about 40 in training – she does not bet.

Her retentive memory was as useful for memorising horses' pedigrees as it was for grasping the essentials of a government proposal, and she quickly accumulated a very extensive knowledge. She kept – and still keeps – in her study a book containing the pedigrees of many thousands of horses, and she decides which stallions and mares will be mated as well as choosing, before the start of each flat season, the races in which each of her horses in training will compete. She has always kept these records up to date herself, and it can be assumed that poring over the lists of names and statistics has been an important part of the pleasure she derives from doing so. As with the gun dogs that she breeds at Sandringham, so with the horses born and nurtured in her stables. The process takes time, patience and considerable expertise but produces long-term satisfaction and no doubt brings a welcome sense of calm to a very crowded life.

During the 1950s and early 1960s she enjoyed considerable success as an owner. Her first win as Queen was at Newmarket in May 1952, and 1954 was her best year. She was leading owner, as she would be again in 1957. Her horse Aureole won the Coronation Cup as well as the King George VI Stakes, the Queen Elizabeth Cup and the Hardwicke Stakes. He was champion sire in 1960 and again the following year. Her Majesty, though obviously in possession of good resources and good advice, is not in the same league of wealth as a number of billionaire owners, and it is not to be assumed that her horses will triumph as a matter of course. She has, for instance, never had a Derby winner. Nevertheless she is extremely proud of the victories they have won, and during Ascot Week she hosts a luncheon at Windsor for which the table is always decorated with the trophies she has won in the past.

The Queen had retained a great deal of her father's style in the way she reigned. There were no immediate alterations, although the monarchy became – in small ways – more informal during the 1950s. A small but characteristic change was that palace footmen no longer wore in their hair a white 'powder' concocted from flour and water, stiffened with soap and starch. It was difficult to mix, took a long time to apply, smelt unpleasant and when outdoors (think of the weather at the Coronation) ran in the rain. Prince Philip, who considered it 'unmanly', saw it as epitomising the sort of nonsense the monarchy should be throwing overboard. The Queen, always considerate towards her servants, no doubt won their gratitude when she put a stop to it in 1955.

In the same year, the rules that effectively barred divorcees from the Royal Enclosure at Ascot were modified. Public attitudes to divorce were changing as a result of its increasing frequency, for many wartime marriages had not survived the years of peace. This was not, however, a complete climb-down on the part of the Court. The Enclosure was being rebuilt and the new one would accommodate more people. Within it was a small area – the Queen's Lawn – in which the old rules still applied.

The quaintly pleasant custom of Royal Bounty, dating from Victoria's reign, was discontinued in 1957. The sovereign had paid £3 and £4 to the parents of triplets and quads respectively, provided that they were all healthy and their parents were married. Another form of Royal bounty was the giving of Maundy money. This – a symbolic annual gift to the poor from the sovereign – was a moribund ancient custom revived by George V and held only in London, on the Thursday before Easter. In 1957 the Maundy service was held at St Albans Abbey, and in subsequent years at Durham, Carlisle, Coventry, Ely and other places. As a means of making the monarch visible to a wider range of her subjects, it proved a great success.

The Levees, which had been such a fixture of previous reigns, had already gone. They had ended with the outbreak of war and it was decided not to revive them. These had been occasions on which people of suitable social or professional standing could apply to attend St James's Palace in formal

'Levee Dress' (civilian men wore a black velvet tailcoat and knee-britches). Here, they shuffled in line towards the throne, bowed to the sovereign and passed on. In their place – and this was a noteworthy innovation – was instituted a series of regular luncheons, at which people who had made some contribution to national life were invited to meet the Queen and Prince Philip informally – if anything that involves footmen and bowing can be described as informal. These began in May 1956 and early guests included the editor of *The Times*, the Bishop of London, the Headmaster of Eton, the managing director of Wembley Stadium and the chairman of the National Coal Board. Although most of them were Establishment figures, the guest list has been highly varied over subsequent years and has brought the Queen in touch with a range of important opinion. They continue during the months of March, May, June, October and December, and they take place on Tuesdays or Thursdays. There are 12 people there, of whom seven are guests. The others are Her Majesty, Prince Philip, the Master of the Household, the Deputy Master and a lady-in-waiting. Those who have attended these testify to the Queen's ability as a hostess to put her guests at ease. They are carefully chosen and matched. The Queen will have read about them in advance, as usual. She knows that for some of them it is difficult to relax in such company or surroundings and she is very good at chairing conversation and ensuring that everyone is involved.

Another casualty of the 1950s was the presentation of debutantes at Court. It was announced in 1957 that the custom was to end the following year. This had been a much more important occasion than the Levees. Presentations were the major event of a young woman's 'coming out', something enjoyed, hated or viewed with impatience by the girls themselves, and cherished by their mothers. It had been said that Prince Philip, who attended the presentations, only smiled at the ugly ones. With the ending of presentations at Court a major headache for London's drivers was removed. For generations, afternoon traffic in the Mall had been held up by the crawling line of vehicles taking the young ladies and their parents to the Palace. A related change was that Trooping the Colour – which, by tradition, had always been held on the second Thursday in June – was moved in 1958 to the second Saturday, so that it would no longer add to weekday congestion. One wonders if there was any connection between the Queen's wartime experiences of driving in the London rush-hour and this consideration for motorists!

Presentations were replaced by an additional Palace garden party, which was added to the two already held each summer. These had been instituted in the 1860s by Queen Victoria, and for almost a century only members of Society attended them. Queen Elizabeth decided that a wider circle of people should have the opportunity, and invitations have since then been issued to organisations, companies, schools, the Civil Service and regiments. About 9,000 people at a time (90 per cent of those invited accept), the men clad mostly in rented finery, spend the hours between four and six in the afternoon wandering the Palace gardens, listening to band-music or crowding the avenue that is cut through the crowd to allow the Queen and her husband to pass. There are three tents in the grounds: one for the Royals, one for the public and one for diplomats. There is another garden party, held in June, at Holyrood in Edinburgh, where the procedure is the same. Guests devour a tea (they consume 20,000 sandwiches) provided by Lyons, the caterers, and in the early years were offered strawberries and cream as well, although this was given up as too expensive. An American, impressed by the custom, once commented that at home, 'Presidents only do this sort of thing when they're running for re-election, and then you know they want something from you.' The Queen does not need her people's votes, yet she gives hospitality anyway. It has proved a most successful innovation.

And yet another change was the televising of the Christmas broadcast. These were begun, on wireless, by George V in 1932. His son had hated them and so did his granddaughter. The speeches were made live on the afternoon of Christmas Day, and understandably ruined the holiday for the sovereign, who could not relax until they had been got over with. Elizabeth did not want to go on television – knowing that she has limited gifts as a public speaker and has difficulty injecting into her scripted words any sense of spontaneity. She gamely did it anyway, as she has ever since, although at least from 1960 it was possible to pre-record it.

The upbringing of the Queen's children was from the beginning different to her own experience, and this too was an innovation. Although if either of them walked past a sentry he would present arms, they did not receive the same level of deference that their mother had known. The Queen told Palace staff that they need not bow and curtsy to her children until they were older, and need not address them as 'Royal Highness'. Their Christian names would be used instead.

It was also a novelty that Prince Charles started school as an ordinary pupil, first at Hill House in Chelsea and then at his father's old prep school, Cheam. The press staked out this school and for a short time besieged it with cameramen. Such attention had not, of course, been a problem in previous reigns when royal children had been educated out of sight behind palace walls. The Queen had to summon Fleet Street editors and ask them, in exchange for a single press opportunity at the school, to leave Charles in peace. The point of sending him to school had been to give him some chance to experience a normal education. The interest it provoked, however, threatened to negate any advantages. The public expectation was in any case that the Queen's children would go to school like other people's, even if their education was private. The notion of royal children being taught at home, as the Queen and Princess Margaret had been only 20 years earlier, now seemed absurdly out of date.

These changes may seem cosmetic – mere tinkering at the edges – when seen in context of the reign as a whole, but at the time they were noticed and appreciated as evidence that the monarchy was updating. The notion of a new and young sovereign, assisted by a husband who was known to be keen on technology and innovation, and somewhat impatient with flummery, was welcomed by much of the public. It fitted the age of jet engines and space exploration. Members of the public, questioned on their attitudes to the monarch, were often impressed: 'She's done away with a lot of the pomp and ceremony,' said one. 'She's a lot more modern in her ideas and a lot more democratic.' Another commented that: 'Nowadays royalty are very different. They're one of us.'

Another innovation of the decade was the advent of outright criticism of the monarch. Attacks in the press on the King or Queen had been commonplace in Hanoverian times, and had also been directed at the eldest son of Queen Victoria both before and after he became King. George V had been characterised as 'dull' by the writer H. G. Wells and, while there could be little arguing with this, his worthiness and sense of duty endeared him to the public. The misdemeanours of Edward VIII were largely unreported and his successor, George VI, was extremely popular. There was thus no recent precedent for personal attacks on the monarch, and Queen Elizabeth was dutiful and conscientious enough not to merit strong criticism. Nevertheless she had from the beginning of her reign courted rebuke by leaving her children for long periods while travelling abroad. She was known to put duty before family, and therefore this was to be expected. However it was also known that, on the night Prince Charles was rushed to Great Ormond Street Hospital for an emergency appendectomy, his mother had stayed at home in bed.

This was mere sniper-fire in comparison with the broadsides

that were suddenly to come, although the attacks were not directed at the Queen's personality or her attitude to her role, but were intended as friendly advice. Lord Altrincham, writing in 1957 in the *National and English Review*, blamed her advisors for the public image she projected as 'a priggish schoolgirl' whose cut-glass, public speaking voice was 'frankly, a pain in the neck', and her speeches – none of which expressed thoughts of her own – were 'prim little sermons': 'Like her mother she appears unable to string even a few sentences together without a written text.' He went on to say, in words that have been remembered ever since: 'The personality conveyed by the utterances that are put into her mouth are those of a priggish schoolgirl, captain of the hockey team, a prefect and recent candidate for confirmation.' Ironically, Elizabeth had only ever been the last of these. He also castigated her Court for its snobbish remoteness and – in a foretaste of one of our own age's most tiresome preoccupations – its lack of 'diversity'. The author was appealing to the Queen to soften her image, but his views provoked a furious backlash from monarchists. The town of Altrincham in Cheshire dissociated itself from him and asked that his title be removed. He was also attacked in the street.

A similar tone was taken by the editor and broadcaster Malcolm Muggeridge in an article for the *Saturday Evening Post*. This was, of course, an American publication, and the British therefore did not initially have easy access to the text. They read quotations in their own press, and were so infuriated that Muggeridge was inundated with threatening and abusive letters. He had, as well as seeing the monarchy as obsolete and snobbish, described the Royal Family as a 'kind of soap opera', a notion that has since become entirely commonplace and, it might be argued, has contributed to its popularity.

Although there was no official reply to the charges, there were lessons to be learned by the Palace about dealing with the press. Access to the family by the media was controlled very strictly. The Palace Press Officer was Commander Richard Colville, a former naval officer with a bluff, quarterdeck manner. He considered the family's private life – and indeed many aspects of their official life – to be none of the public's business, and earned the nickname 'the abominable no-man' for his repeated refusals to answer questions or confirm information: 'That is a private matter. I can't help at all.' He was to be the last such official employed by the Press Office. There would soon be a change of attitude.

Many people felt that the young Queen was breathing fresh air into a moribund institution. There was a perception that she was surrounded by dinosaurs, who, because they actually ran her Household and filled her appointments book, ensured that she remained stuck in the past. Sixty years later, the perception of a visitor to the Palace would still be that the Queen's staff are, in Altrincham's phrase, 'tweedy and plummy'. There is no denying this, but why should it matter? It is a close-knit working environment in which the shared backgrounds of officials and their families mean that they can work well together. Those – and they include most of the ceremonial posts at Court – who are, or were, senior officers in the Services have by definition qualifications that are highly suitable. Military training or background provides familiarity with ceremonial, orders and graded hierarchy, it implies proven loyalty to the Crown, an ability to organise large groups of people efficiently and to think fast if some emergency requires an improvised solution. They are unlikely ever to pose a security risk or to talk to the press.

Whatever a few errant subjects thought of her at home, the Queen had proved her value abroad, where the New Elizabethan image had become unstuck. The invasion of Egypt by French, British and Israeli troops to seize control of the Suez Canal in 1956 had proved a major humiliation. The operation had been cynical and ill-conceived, and America refused to support it. It was called off and the soldiers evacuated.

Towards America the British public had considerably bruised feelings. They had already had to accept that they were now a second-rank power, but they believed they were still capable of greatness and of international influence. They felt entitled to American respect, if not active support. The USA felt that Britain had brought catastrophe on herself by embarking on such a rash adventure in the first place. The following autumn, the Queen made a state visit to the USA – the 350th anniversary of the founding of Virginia made a handy excuse – to restore good relations.

It is at these moments that Royalty comes into its own. Not officially connected with the government's foreign policy, and therefore never to blame for mistakes, it can appeal instead entirely to the intangible but important areas of sentiment and culture. The visit was a greater success than anyone could have predicted. It was the Americans' first chance to see the young Queen, and they were charmed – as others had been – by her combination of personal shyness and official gravity. She was given a ticker-tape parade in New York, and greeted by a huge turnout in Washington. No modern American president has yet declined to be seen with British Royalty, and Eisenhower was in any case an old wartime acquaintance. Delighted by this reception, she was willing to set aside a certain amount of formality. The press at home noticed that she had been at close quarters – almost mingling – with crowds and one paper, the *Daily Herald*, asked: 'People here have been reading of the Queen going about freely among ordinary people, behaving like an ordinary person. Canada loved it. America was bowled over by it. Why is it not allowed to happen here?'

Seeing the enthusiasm of crowds that greeted her, an American commentator observed: 'There goes Britain's ultimate diplomatic weapon.' She had saved Anglo-American relations during a very sticky patch, refocusing attention on the two countries' shared heritage instead of their divergent world-views. There is between the British monarchy and the American public a very warm relationship. It goes back not to 1957, or 1951 – her own first visit – nor even to 1939, when her parents went to the USA in an attempt to win sympathy in the coming war. It originated in the first such visit, by the Prince of Wales (later Edward VII) in 1860, which was a good-will tour without ulterior motive. Since that time the British monarchy has considered the American public worth meeting and befriending. They also genuinely love the country, whose people – despite their republican past and present – have never shown them anything but the deepest kindness. Their visits have enabled those Americans who wish to do so to feel that they, too, are part of the magic.

As well as being instrumental in sealing good relations with the West's great superpower, the queen was also deployed in the Cold War against the Communist world. Her visit to Ghana soon after its independence in 1957 was both a personal and a symbolic triumph, helping to turn opinion among regional rulers away from Moscow. The Soviet Union saw Africa as an important ideological battleground, and was able to throw around a good deal of Marxist rhetoric that resonated with the peoples there. Ghana was unstable and ruled by a president, Kwame Nkrumah, whose autocratic style had made him unpopular. He was sufficiently unpopular, in fact, to be the likely target of assassination, and thus put at risk anyone in his company. He had become a tireless – even meddling – champion of anti-imperialism, and was loud in his condemnation of the colonial power that the Queen personified, so Her Majesty might well have expected an awkward meeting. Despite these factors she went ahead with the visit, and Nkrumah was delighted. Her appearance with him added to his standing with his people, increasing perception of him as an international statesman. Britain had just given independence to Ghana – hardly the act of an oppressor – and the fact that its ruler visited in person made a very positive impression on the people. They crowded to look at her at every opportunity and, when she discovered that they were disappointed not to see her wearing more jewellery, she obliged by putting on in public every stone she had available. One could not imagine Khrushchev being able to compete with that!

# MATURITY, 1960–1970

'The English are getting bored with their monarchy.'

By the beginning of the 1960s the Queen had, as she had put it, 'matured into' her office. Her apprenticeship was long over, with her family growing up and her two children starting on their own life's-journeys. Her habits were well established, the year divided between London, Windsor, Norfolk, Edinburgh and Aberdeenshire. She would be less newsworthy, for the press had had a decade in which to chronicle her tastes and her movements and was surely running out of subject matter. She and Philip were on the verge of middle life and, as he put it: 'I would have thought that we're entering the least interesting period of our kind of glamorous existence.' The Royal Family, in other words, expected to be given more privacy because neither they nor their functions were any longer remarkable. Public opinion seemed to agree, and viewing-figures for the Christmas broadcast were declining. 'The English,' the now-infamous Malcolm Muggeridge told an American television interviewer, 'are getting bored with their monarchy.'

Far from fading into obscurity, the Queen aroused widespread interest by having two more children, Andrew (1960) and Edward (1964). The media did not, however, have the field-day over these new arrivals that might have been expected. Her Majesty decided that this second pair of Royal children should have greater privacy than their older siblings – or she herself – had enjoyed. Access to them was deliberately not allowed to journalists and photographers during the earliest part of their lives. In the case of Prince Andrew, he was not seen by the public until a month after he was born, and this fuelled rumours that he was in some way abnormal.

The iconoclasm of the 1950s continued into the new decade. The Establishment – any institution that exercised power or owed its prestige to the past – was fair game for satirists. The most wounding blows to the established order were, however, self-inflicted. The discovery that two young upper-class diplomats, Guy Burgess and Donald Maclean, had been spying for the Soviet Union was made when both of them defected. A third man, Anthony Blunt, was Surveyor of the Queen's Pictures, although his connection to the others would not be revealed until many years later. The Profumo scandal occurred in 1963. A government minister was caught in a sexual liaison that compromised national security, and then lied about his involvement in the House of Commons. Both of these incidents suggested the same thing – that the class which had traditionally assumed the leadership of the country, and justified its position on grounds of birth and education, was no longer to be trusted. As a setback to national confidence these things were worse even than Suez, for here the rot was shown to be within. It was even rumoured that the birth of the Queen's youngest son, Prince Edward, was deliberately planned to counter this collective despair.

The monarchy, with its ostentatious public ceremonies, was the most highly visible aspect of the Establishment, and as the social upheavals of the decade gathered pace it was perceived as increasingly irrelevant and outdated. Not only had the governing class failed the country, they were being rendered irrelevant by the arrival of a thrusting new meritocratic culture. The capital was dubbed 'Swinging London' (a phrase coined by *Time* magazine) and Guardsmens' tunics began to be seen, worn unbuttoned, on long-haired civilians. The appeal of ancient ceremony – at least to the young, who dominated virtually all culture – was much diminished. The Labour Government under Harold Wilson that came to power in 1964 reflected this trend, and the following year did away with hereditary peerages, while conferring honours on the footballer Stanley Matthews and on The Beatles. In these uncharted cultural waters the Royals lost their status as reference-point for taste, dress, manners (they would not regain influence in matters of style until the advent of Diana 20 years later). The 'role models' to whom millions looked were no longer the tight-lipped, dutiful members of the Royal Family but a galaxy of brash and publicity-seeking musicians, photographers and comedians.

Interestingly, at precisely the time that this new Establishment was succeeding the old one, the Royals made a connection with it. Princess Margaret had found happiness with a photographer, Antony Armstrong-Jones, and married him at Westminster Abbey in February 1960. Her flamboyant, theatrical personality fitted well with his circle of creative friends. With her long-standing curiosity about life outside the palace railings, she was delighted to experience evenings cooking and dining, tête-à-tête, in the shabby rooms in Rotherhithe where he lived. Her friendship and subsequent marriage to 'Tony' – who had taken portraits of the Royals – was initially very happy and brought the monarchy into the same social orbit as the likes of Peter Sellers and Mick Jagger. This connection was not universally welcome. Prince Philip (the Queen had by now made him a British Prince) and his new brother-in-law were entirely incompatible personalities, and Courtiers regarded him – despite his Eton and Cambridge background – as a tradesman. Nevertheless, his presence within the Family for most of two decades was to give the pinnacle of the Establishment a stake in the new era. The *Daily Mirror* was to report gleefully in 1965 that Sellers and Spike Milligan, stalwarts of the extremely zany *Goon Show*, had attended the queen's birthday party.

The advent of a new cultural mindset was not the only thing that caused Royalty to lose some of its distance from the public, however. The tabloid media had by now got into its stride, and the behaviour of the Family was examined more closely. With their frequent travels, the children's schooling and the parties attended by Princess Margaret, there was plenty to write about, and newspaper readers became increasingly judgemental about the Royals. The sense of humour – or offhand rudeness, according to one's perspective – of the Queen's husband became so well-known that a book of his sayings – *The Wit of Prince Philip* – was published. It seemed, after all, that public interest was not going to evaporate anytime soon.

Young, energetic, attractive and photogenic, the Royal Family had become a staple of the illustrated papers, much as – in America – the Kennedys were at the same time. The coverage given to the Queen and her children significantly furthered the notion of the Royals as an average family. In previous reigns, pictures of the Family when off duty had tended to show them shooting, a decidedly upper-class activity, pursued amid the cheerless winter landscapes of Norfolk or the Highlands, and which they followed – judging by their humourless expressions – without much pleasure. Their tailored tweeds and Purdey shotguns were well beyond the financial reach of most of their subjects. Now the sovereign, her husband and children were pictured having picnics on Scottish beaches without a servant in sight, dressed in clothes that were old, comfortable and just like other peoples'. A woman enthused that: 'It's lovely to see them on holiday. They wear the sort of things I wear – an old skirt and coat, when they are in Scotland.'

At this time national prosperity was increasing, disposable income was greater and the result was a more noticeable social levelling. The visible differences between classes blurred – especially with a tendency of the upper echelons to dress down – and the public expected those in positions of privilege to be less remote and nearer to themselves. A poll found that three out of five people 'wanted the Royal Family to live more like ordinary people'.

Although they lived in the Palace during the week, the place in which they relaxed at weekends was Windsor. They had had one part of the Castle – the Edward III Tower – renovated and made into a simple and modern dwelling. Hugh Casson designed the interiors, which were hung with paintings by artists such as Edward Seago and Sidney Nolan. The notion was that these premises would be self-catering, though in fact there were always staff in attendance. Nevertheless they achieved a sense of informality and simple comfort that could never be found amid the ponderous, grand, inherited furnishings of other rooms in the Castle. Although the press would love to have photographed it, this was and remained an entirely private domain, a sort of holiday hideaway which happened to be in the midst of a very busy castle that was thronging with tourists.

The Queen had always seen Windsor as her home, Buckingham Palace as her office and the other residences as seasonal retreats. No other place evokes the same affection as Windsor – the biggest inhabited castle in the world, and by far the oldest Royal residence. She not only enjoyed spending weekends there but decided, in 1964, that Christmas would in future be celebrated there instead of at Sandringham. This practice was to last until 1988, when the Family once again made Norfolk their home during the festive season.

Christmas among the Royals is a major event. It begins with the taping of the Queen's broadcast. Until 1957 this was made on radio. It was then given live on television until 1960, at which time it became possible to pre-record. This not only avoided ruining Her Majesty's Christmas Day but meant that the film could be sent to Commonwealth countries in time for 25 December. The broadcasts, always played at three p.m. on the day, are watched in the Royal household too. The programmes take the form of a survey of the previous 12 months, and enable the Queen to give personal reactions to events. Although she is in a domestic setting – the fact that she is speaking from her home suggests intimacy – and though the thoughts are her own, her delivery is still formal for she is reciting prepared remarks (when once asked to be more spontaneous, she retorted: 'I'm not an actress!').

She gives a Christmas tree to several institutions, such as St Paul's Cathedral and the Royal Hospital. She also gives a present, and a Christmas pudding, to every member of her staff. A ball is held for them, taking place in alternate years at the Palace or at Windsor.

The entire family gathers for Christmas, including all the cousins – the Kents and Gloucesters and Ogilvys. The opening of gifts is actually held on the night of Christmas Eve, a reflection of the Family's Germanic past, for it was Prince Albert who introduced many of their particular customs. Long tables have been set up, divided so that each person has their own pile of presents. The tree comes from the Sandringham Estate and the decorations, as in many families, are heirlooms.

On the day itself the morning is devoted to church. All the Royals are present, not only because it is considered a duty but because the media will be there in force, the occasion will be extensively photographed and the image of them, united in worship, is important. A lengthy lunch follows, but must be finished before three o'clock, when the Family watches the queen's address in respectful silence. The evening is spent in somewhat riotous party games, the most popular of which is charades. It is well known that the Queen excels at this. Despite her outburst that 'I am not an actress!' she apparently does have considerable talent for mimicry and for doing impressions of prime ministers, world leaders and other notables with whom she has come in contact. One hopes this is true.

The Queen had, apparently, always wanted four children. The first two had been born before she came to the throne, and after she had become a reigning monarch there was simply not time for others (though this had not stopped Queen Victoria, who had nine!). The fact that she was able to resume motherhood in the 1960s was another sign that she had settled into her role. The experience of the younger pair was to be different to that of their siblings. Neither was to be treated with the same rigour that Charles experienced; indeed, both would be relatively indulged.

Relative indulgence, however, did not mean either mountains of toys or licence to misbehave. All four children were brought up in the care of strict nursery staff and under the equally stern eye of their parents. All of them would quickly have learned that their behaviour mattered because they were so much in the public eye. Their father taught them to be punctiliously polite, not least to servants, and they would be sent to apologise to any whom they were heard to address rudely. With his financially austere youth and Gordonstoun background, Philip was also unlikely to indulge the wants of his offspring, though he could be a very affectionate parent. The Queen had also had a comparatively simple childhood, but was in any case known to be possessed of a thrifty streak that would not have sat comfortably with the notion of extravagance.

The Queen deferred to her husband in the matter of their children's upbringing. He was head of the family, and she wished him to make the decisions that involved their private rather than their public life. The fact that he could be tough, impatient and demanding was, she felt, necessary. She shared his view, for instance, that Charles was too sensitive, and she therefore made no attempt to protect him against Philip's often loud disapproval. As a parent, she was different from her own mother and father. There was no question of mollycoddling her offspring with an artificially conjured arcadia. They were sent to school rather than protected behind Palace walls. Since three of her own children were boys and the fourth a tomboy, the atmosphere in which they grew up was in any case entirely unlike that at Royal Lodge. There is truth in the notion that she was a distant parent, but distant does not mean unaffectionate, and it is worth stressing that she was highly attentive within the limits her official life allowed. She greatly enjoyed motherhood. With all her children she had devoted time to them every day (she and Philip always bathed them in the evenings), and she had put back by half an hour her weekly Tuesday evening audience with the Prime Minister because it clashed with their bedtime. She could not, however, afford to make them the highest priority in her life. She was far busier during their growing years than any normal mother, and it was a matter of simple duty with her that her job always came first. This attitude was bred into her and explains why she was willing to go on a six-month Commonwealth tour while her first children were still small. Whatever her personal feelings, they must be subordinate to her position, for she would be letting down millions by not fulfilling her function.

A thoughtful, sensitive and often timid child, Charles was by now an adolescent, and was in many ways the antithesis of his father, who had sought to instil in him a toughness that was not in his nature. Charles's response had been to draw closer to his grandmother. The Queen Mother had early noticed in him a shyness reminiscent of her husband, and had always been his ally. In 1962 he went to school at Gordonstoun. Although he knew something of it through his father, the culture shock would have been considerable. A non-academic school whose objective was character-building rather than exam passes, the isolation of its Highland setting was matched by a spartan lifestyle that emphasised adventure training and self-reliance, a quality pursued through cold showers, unheated dormitories and cross-country runs in all weathers. One reason it was chosen for him – and the decision was not made lightly – was that it was thought to represent a classless community, or at any rate one more socially varied than a traditional private school in England would have been.

It had suited Philip extremely well, developing his qualities of leadership, but it was entirely the wrong place for a boy of Charles's nature. His father had thought it would increase his toughness. In fact it drove him further into his shell. He was bullied, especially on the sports field where other boys could deliberately tackle him. Instead of being befriended by the socially ambitious, the opposite happened – he was shunned by boys who feared accusations of toadying. As well as this, the school put him in direct comparison with Prince Philip, a contest he could only lose since the ethos favoured his father's qualities and not his own. He was deeply unhappy, and reluctant to return at the beginning of each term. An important motive for selecting a school many hundreds of miles from Fleet Street was that it offered a greater chance of privacy and normality. Even this was compromised, however, when on a visit to Stornoway he was driven by curious crowds to take refuge in a hotel bar and, at a loss, to order a cherry brandy. The press, which had agreed to leave him in peace during his schooldays, found this too good an opportunity to miss, and represented him as an under-age drinker. The incident clouded his schooldays because – given that he was otherwise left alone by the media – it became the only thing that people knew about him. Even though he had some eventual success at school, becoming 'Keeper', or head boy, as his father had done, he left the school without regret and was to send his own sons elsewhere. By the time his brothers followed him to Gordonstoun, conditions had changed. Dormitories were no longer freezing, the regime was less hearty, and in Edward's time there were even girl pupils. Not being direct heirs to the throne the others suffered less, perhaps, from the attitudes that had bedevilled Charles.

Unlike her brother, Anne had needed no grandmotherly support. She had inherited her uncomplicated, no-nonsense nature direct from Philip with virtually no modification. She would grow up to be extrovert, practical and blunt, sharing his habit of snapping at reporters, if not his intelligent interest in science and technology. She was sent to Benenden, a traditional girls' school in Kent. Confident and outgoing, she thrived in the sociable atmosphere, and became popular. With no academic ambitions, she developed instead what was to be her lifelong passion for riding and eventing. She honed her skills in this while at the school, and went on to combine them successfully with the duties her position required.

The Queen was naturally interested in her children's progress, and proud of their achievements, but she believed her husband knew best as regards their upbringing and she was not noticeably sympathetic towards Charles. She is, in any case, a self-contained personality who does not believe in being demonstrative. It is part of what she is and what has made her so enormously successful as a monarch. As her children had grown up and attracted comment or behaved in ways that were unfortunate, she preferred to avoid confrontation and was inclined to let them alone, not 'micro-managing' their lives as her own mother had done. She will, to this day, hear no criticism of them and this is especially true of Andrew, the one of whom she is fondest.

The Queen's official life continued to be busy. Among her visitors were the Kennedys. Both the charismatic young President and his wife had previous connections with the Royal Family. His father had been American Ambassador – if not a very successful one – just before the war, and his mother and sisters had been presented at Court. Mrs Kennedy, formerly a photojournalist, had been sent to cover the Coronation for

American newspapers. They were in London for a family christening – Jackie's sister lived there – and were on the return journey to Washington from Paris, where she had received a tumultuous welcome and a great deal of media coverage. This adulation now spilled over to London, where immense crowds gathered to catch a glimpse of her. The Kennedys were invited to dinner by the Queen and, although civilities were exchanged, it is unlikely that Her Majesty was as taken with the First Lady as Parisians had been. The Queen did not wish to have her thunder stolen by a woman who – the mere spouse of a Head of State – was attracting too much publicity. Mrs Kennedy also represented a Hollywood type of glamour that has always been anathema to the Queen. A few years afterward, when the notion of a television programme on royal palaces was first mooted, it was suggested that Her Majesty conduct the audience through the different rooms herself. The Queen, referring to a televised tour of the White House which the President's wife had previously hosted, snapped 'I'm not Jackie Kennedy.' Nevertheless the assassination in Dallas sent shock waves through the United Kingdom, and the Queen gave permission for flags to be flown at half-mast across London, while her Guardsmen wore black armbands on their uniforms. She was later to dedicate a permanent memorial – an acre of ground at Runnymede – to the President's memory and to share the occasion with his widow and children.

In domestic affairs, Britain underwent a significant change when in 1964 the Conservative Government was narrowly beaten in the general election, and for the first time since her accession she found herself dealing with a Labour Prime Minister. Harold Wilson was a decade older than the Queen, a Yorkshireman who, as was commonplace in his Party, made a virtue of his impoverished background (he once had to apologise to the Commons for exaggerating it). A former Oxford economics don, he had little in common with Her Majesty. Every one of the men who had previously attended weekly audiences with her – Churchill, Eden, Macmillan, Douglas-Home – had come from a hinterland of aristocracy, public school and familiarity with the pastimes of royalty. Wilson was a new departure, yet he found the meetings a pleasure. The Queen, it seemed, enjoyed a change as much as anyone else. She was curious about his background and his politics, which were understandably different to those of many who surrounded her. She knew a great deal about his party and about the Commons, so they could 'talk shop' without difficulty. With his teaching experience he was gifted at explaining things, he had a good sense of humour and an agreeable manner. Their genuine rapport was demonstrated by the fact that his audiences often overran the customary 20–30 minutes. He was delighted to hear that she looked forward to these visits. He, in turn, greatly enjoyed staying with her at Balmoral. His memories were not to be the negative reaction of a socialist politician to a shooting-and-fishing country estate or the pitfalls of observing upper-class etiquette, but of the informality and friendliness of the Queen. Accustomed to seeing her at audiences or state occasions, he was enchanted to find her cooking, washing dishes and driving herself about, and to find that he fitted in after all. Although she would one day answer the question of who was her favourite among her premiers with the words: 'Winston, of course. It was always so much fun,' Wilson undoubtedly loomed very large in her affections. In April 1976 she and Prince Philip were to attend his retirement dinner at Number Ten, a gesture she had not made for any Prime Minister but Churchill.

Because the Queen is the pinnacle of the social structure, and has a lifestyle and tastes that reflect those of the senior aristocracy, it might be assumed that she is conservative in politics. She is without doubt *socially* conservative – yet she never betrays a flicker of party favouritism and she enjoyed her contact with Labour premiers and Cabinet ministers. Why? Because she is genuinely apolitical and therefore does not hold against them their views or their party loyalties. Secondly, because she admires – and is interested to meet – people who have risen through the ranks of politics. They offer a perspective that she finds refreshing, and offer a point of contact with a world she cannot enter. Thirdly, she perhaps takes quiet satisfaction in knowing how well she can get on with people from outside the class into which she was born, but then her grandfather had a very good rapport with Ramsay MacDonald, the first Labour premier, so there is a family precedent. Since she would hate revolution or serious social upheaval, she may also enjoy the knowledge that she can gently woo left-wing firebrands nearer the middle ground. This has been well known in the Labour Party for generations. Richard Crossman, once Minister of Education, wrote that: 'The nearer the Queen they get the more the working-class members of Cabinet love her and she loves them.' She worked with her first labour Government skilfully and well.

She had more trouble, in fact, with the Commonwealth. In May 1961 South Africa, scene of her 21st birthday, became a republic and was forced to leave the organisation because of its racial policy. Its neighbour, Rhodesia, declared itself unilaterally independent four years later in order to maintain white minority rule. In Quebec, there were loud rumblings in favour of separation from the Canadian Federation and therefore from the Queen, who was to visit the province in 1964. It was stated in the press on both sides of the Atlantic that there was a plot to assassinate her and that this would be 'a second Dallas'. She herself displayed the usual combination of courage and fatalism, letting it be known that: 'I am not worried about the visit. We are quite relaxed.' In the event she could afford to be, for the security operation was massive and any potential troublemakers were controlled very carefully. She encountered nothing more serious than a few displays of deliberate rudeness.

Throughout the 1960s the British Empire was being wound up throughout Africa and the West Indies. Independence ceremonies that looked much the same when seen on Pathe newsreels – with the lowering of the Union Flag at midnight and the raising of the new national one – became so common that the press began to lose interest. Each occasion was attended by some member of the Family, and even cousins were roped in to help (The Duke of Kent: British Guiana; his wife, the Duchess: Uganda). The alternative to British rule was not severance of all ties but the choice of maintaining cultural links, even in the case of a sovereign state, through membership of the Commonwealth (now called the Commonwealth of Nations rather than the British Commonwealth). There were distinct advantages, such as priority access to overseas aid from the United Kingdom, but there was also the kudos of contact with the Queen. She regularly attended the conference for Commonwealth Heads of Government. She recognised them, held meetings with them, chatted informally at social gatherings, remembered the names of their wives, had her picture taken with them. Images of them with Royalty and with other leaders naturally enhanced their prestige at home. They were also able to 'network' among themselves. The Premiers of small and uninfluential countries met on equal terms with those of large and powerful ones. It was, as it still is, a statesman's club that attracts the envy of many outside. Were it not for the personal interest of the British monarch, it might well have met less regularly and died of neglect before it had had the chance to mature and increase. In the decades that followed she would go further in her attachment: the Conference would no longer be held invariably in Britain but in different venues throughout the world. No matter where it was, she and the Duke would attend it regularly.

In spite of international upheaval and official duty, the public continued to see – or wish to see – the Royals as a mirror-image of themselves. The popular press had become steadily more intrusive, and the Palace had realised that aloofness was not the answer when dealing with this. Better to accommodate them where possible, and thus have some influence over what they published. Public relations took a significant step forward when, in 1965, William Heseltine was appointed Assistant Press Secretary. An Australian – and thus free from accusations that his background or attitudes were stereotypically aloof – he managed the balancing trick of being respected by both the monarch (who found him invaluable) and the media. He was gently and tactfully to persuade the Family that some greater accommodation of general curiosity would help them. In the new climate of media relations that he built, the Queen granted permission for television networks to visit her homes. This was not something she would willingly have done – she is a jealous guardian of her privacy – but two others within her circle helped convince her that the notion would delight the public. One was Lord Mountbatten, a man with little to learn about the art of self-promotion. The other was his son-in-law, the film-maker Lord Brabourne. Mountbatten had just taken part in a series about his life that was shown on national television. It was widely watched, and he was very pleased with it. He felt that the royal homes of Britain would not only make gripping television but would give a hint of the life of the monarch in a way that would intrigue her subjects. Although reluctant, Her Majesty agreed.

The series *Royal Palaces of Britain* was produced in 1966 by both television networks, BBC and ITV, together. This was a look at six residences, and was shown on Christmas Day that year. The programmes proved, as expected, immensely popular. It really created a sense of privilege that, as the publicity material announced: 'By kind permission of the Queen, cameras [are] allowed to enter into the private apartments of Britain's Royal Palaces for the first time.' It enabled her subjects to look behind the scenes at buildings they knew well by sight, and allowed incidental glances at the tastes of the Royal Family. The success of this venture soon gave birth to a bolder idea –

a further documentary, this time not about the buildings but their inhabitants.

The result was not seen for a further three years. Simply titled *Royal Family*, although the press was to nickname it *Corgi and Beth*, it used a formula that was to be repeated often in both books and exhibitions – that of following the Queen for a year in order to record the activities that were typical of her life and work. Several scenes assumed special interest, and stayed in the collective memory. One showed the Family cooking in the open air at Balmoral (Prince Philip, it transpired, had designed the barbecue equipment himself, and presided over it with his usual air of command). Another depicted the Queen visiting a local shop to buy sweets for Prince Edward. The exchange of money, and pleasantries, looked natural enough – although, of course, an entire camera crew had had to squeeze into the small premises, too, and it was later claimed that because the Queen carries no money, one of them had had to lend her the necessary coinage.

The film took 75 days to shoot, and the result was vivid, informative and illuminating. Most who saw it were fascinated by these unprecedented glimpses of the private moments of such a public family, though there was also a surprising amount of hand-wringing by traditionalists, who felt that the monarchy was diminished by showing them on holiday looking much like anyone's next-door neighbours. Once again, there was astonishment at how, when relaxing, they could seem so ordinary. Viewers were also impressed to see something of the mechanics of how the Household was run, how hard the Queen worked and what she did all day. The programme was shown twice – once by each network – during the month of June 1969, and was watched by something like two-thirds of all Britons. Those sitting enthralled by their television sets included, apparently, a professional house-breaker, who wrote anonymously to the producers that he had stayed at home from work in order to watch. The programme was sold to 140 countries and earned £120,000 in profits, which were divided between the Queen and the BBC. Her Majesty agreed to donate her share to the Society of Film and Television Arts.

*Royal Family* greatly increased public interest in the monarchy. It was a most effective riposte to Mr Muggeridge's claim. It also, however, set a new standard for intrusiveness. Having had such a privileged look at the private lives of the Queen and her family, the public was to regard such intimacy not as a rare, once-and-for-all glimpse but as normal, and a right. By showing – or suggesting – that the Royals were like everyone else it helped to trivialise them, and was regarded by some within the Family as a disaster. It is significant that the film has remained locked in the Royal Archives ever since. The Queen owns the copyright, and it cannot be shown without her express permission, which is not forthcoming. Although excerpts are occasionally screened the programme in its entirety has, for the present at least, vanished.

The Royals may regret allowing access to their lives through the medium of television, but what else could they have done? Public curiosity about them, as their children grew up, was increasing anyway. The eroding of deference would have happened regardless of whether or not the public could watch them having a barbecue. The result would have been the same, and quite possibly worse. What was to happen would have happened. It was the spirit of the times.

Less than two weeks after the screenings, public attention was again focused on Royalty. Prince Charles, whom his mother had created Prince of Wales in 1958 when he was a schoolboy at Cheam, was now 21 and was to be formally invested as Prince at Caernarvon Castle. This event, the most important ceremony since the Coronation, was an opportunity for Wales to stage a big state occasion. In charge of the arrangements was Antony Armstrong-Jones, who had been created Earl of Snowdon on his marriage to Princess Margaret and was now also Constable of Caernarvon Castle. He had a flair for architectural design – he had provided an imaginative aviary for London Zoo – and established within the castle ruins a strikingly simple but grandiose setting. On the greensward – for the ceremony was entirely out of doors – was a plain circular dais. It was of Welsh slate, as were the three thrones for the Prince and his parents. It was protected from any inclement weather by a swooping canopy but, because the ceremony had to be visible to television cameras at different angles, this was made of transparent Perspex, held up by what looked like giant spears. Striking and very contemporary, but with just the right historic echoes, it looked remarkably like the stage-set for one of the Shakespeare history plays, and was, in fact, created by a theatrical designer. A simple and very modern gold chaplet was made for the Prince – again, this looked rather like a prop from a school play – and he wore the uniform of the recently established Royal Regiment of Wales. Snowdon himself, who would be present in his official capacity, neither had nor wanted any Court costume, and designed for himself a simple but effective suit of dark green velvet.

The ceremony itself was somewhat contrived. For centuries, Princes of Wales had been connected to the Principality in name only. They had assumed their title in London or Windsor without any formalities. Only in 1911 when George V's eldest son (the Duke of Windsor) had been invested had the Welsh Cabinet Minister, Lloyd George, suggested making a public spectacle of it. In 1969, as in 1911, most Welsh were delighted, but this time there was resentment from a noisy element of nationalists, the Free Wales Army, which threatened to disrupt what they saw as the celebration of an alien dynasty's presence in their country. There were bomb threats and even explosions – one device blew off a boy's leg, another killed the man who was setting it. Security was tight as the Royals and government officials and the public descended on the small town, but the weather held, the crowds were enthusiastic, the extremists did no damage that day, and 1 July 1969 entered history.

The decade therefore ended with a flourish for the house of Windsor. They had provided their people with a great set-piece event, and they had increased their popularity by exposure through the media of television. They might have had grounds for complacency.

But in that last year Prince Philip triggered something of a crisis. Interviewed on television while in America, he dropped the bombshell of announcing that the following year the Royal Family would go 'into the red', for the Queen's Civil list allowance of £475,000 a year had not been increased since she came to the throne. He was to follow this by remarking that: 'We may have to move into a smaller home.'

In immediately following years, finance was to play a bigger role for the Royals – and generate more controversy – than anything else.

# JUBILEE, 1970–1980

'She could not believe that people had that much affection for her.'

In many ways this was a decade best forgotten. For the first time large-scale terrorism became a feature of British life, and the level of both viciousness and destruction was altogether shocking. The Ulster troubles, dormant for a generation, had re-surfaced as a direct result of International Human Rights Year in 1968. Catholic campaigning against Protestant discrimination had escalated, by the following summer, into virtual civil war, and made it necessary for troops to back up the police in keeping order. Not since the previous Irish conflict in the 1920s had a part of the United Kingdom seemed so much like the Wild West. Gunshots and explosions were a routine night-time sound in Belfast and Londonderry. With huge amounts of illegal weaponry in the hands of extremists, bombings, shootings, kidnappings and assassinations became so commonplace as to merit only brief media interest. Judges, policemen and indeed anyone linked with the British Government was at daily risk of murder. The British Army's peacekeeping role was effectively the same type of 'police action' that had occupied it for 40 years in Palestine and Cyprus and Aden, and this seemed similarly thankless and unwinnable. The new wave of terrorism, so much nearer home, brought to British cities a degree of violence and carnage not seen since the Blitz. The IRA clearly had the resources and determination to mount a lengthy campaign, and what added an element of despair for the public was the knowledge that there was no feasible solution or hope of an end. As a result there was an ugly, fearful edge to life. People went about their business with a grim determination to carry on, braced for horror and loss.

Industrial relations were to reach their worst level since the Depression. Strikes and shortages were frequent, lengthy and widespread. Trade unions were seen to hold the whip-hand and to bully and victimise the rest of the public. Many people's memories of the 1970s are of power cuts, militant strikers, bombs and rampant inflation. Britain's economic woes became so acute that the Government was obliged to seek a bail-out from the International Monetary Fund, a thing no major developed country would expect to do. To images of families dining at home by torchlight at the time of the three-day week were added those of piled-up, uncollected rubbish during the 'winter of discontent' and of plane-loads of foreigners arriving to strip the shelves of British shops because the exchange rate was so much in their favour. These years were symbolised by the youth cult of Punk, a deliberate and anarchic ugliness that suited Britain's status as the Sick Man of Europe.

The Royal Family was naturally not immune to these conditions. As always their position at the top of the British Establishment made them vulnerable. As a target for terrorists they had a great deal to offer – to kill one of them would guarantee headlines and vast international attention, which is what terrorists want. The loss of one might so horrify the British people that their government would be pressured into conceding defeat. They were not difficult to track, since their movements were listed each day in the Court Circular, and specific events were often announced long months in advance. They did not hide, and were frequently in front of crowds that would give cover to an attacker. When going on horseback to and from Horse Guards for Trooping the Colour the Queen could hardly have been more conspicuous – seated above the heads of the crowd and moving at walking pace. No American President would dream of being so exposed in public, yet the Queen would countenance no significant compromise. She utterly refused to allow anything that gave the impression she or her family were cowed. The only noticeable concession she was to make was in the matter of visits to Northern Ireland, in that these were not reported until they were over.

The Royals were a security nightmare but once again the quiet, dogged courage with which the Queen and her family continued their routine of visits and speeches and ceremonies was resoundingly impressive and reassuring. 'So long as she's carrying on as usual,' people seemed to feel, 'things can't be that bad.' Her Majesty was, after all, something of a veteran in terms of terrorism. There had been IRA bomb threats in her childhood. During the 1950s there had been rumblings of danger from Cypriot activists (near Balmoral, of all places!), and there had been threats from the separatist zealots in Quebec and Wales. Unfortunately, an attitude of business as usual was not always the safest policy, and before the decade was over one senior member of the Family would have been murdered by the IRA.

It was highly ironic that, just as the threat to their personal safety reached unprecedented levels, the Royals also came closer to the people than ever before. 1970 is remembered as the year of the first 'walkabout', a custom that permanently changed the way in which the monarchy was seen by the public, and which the Queen herself saw as the beginning of a new relationship with her subjects. The term was associated with Australian aborigines and used to describe a period spent wandering in the Bush. In this context it meant that the sovereign, and often her family, travelled short distances on foot and stopped to talk to members of the crowd. These are now commonplace, and expected. We are also accustomed, through television, to seeing the Royal Family close up. It is therefore difficult to imagine the impact of this custom on those who were present on the first occasions. The notion of being only inches from the Royals, perhaps catching their eye and being asked a question, of being able to give a bouquet or to have your picture taken talking to them, was a major innovation.

The first walkabout took place in Wellington, New Zealand, in March that year, though the Maltese claim that the Queen made precisely the same sort of informal progress in the streets of Valetta during a visit three years earlier. In Wellington the Queen and Prince Philip, with Charles and Anne, were due to attend a function at the Town Hall. They arrived by car, but instead of simply being driven to the entrance and leaving onlookers with no more than a glimpse of waving glove, they disembarked in the square outside and walked – slowly, for long minutes – all the way round the building to its front door. In the process, thousands of people saw or photographed them, hundreds called out greetings, scores shook their hands and dozens spoke with them. This was no more a spontaneous event than anything the Royals do when on duty. It had been suggested, and planned, by the city authorities as a way of involving local people more closely in the event. The second one took place a few months later in Coventry, and it too was a huge success, setting a pattern that has been followed ever since both at home and overseas. Naturally the royal party would divide a crowd between them, walking on different sides of a street. This was much the same thing they were already doing when meeting the guests at a Palace garden party. It was an effective way of ensuring that onlookers felt some sense of contact with them, though it could be unfortunate if people were audibly disappointed with the one they got.

In a sense, this new form of encounter between sovereign and people was asking for trouble. It made life extremely difficult for security staff to have the Queen moving slowly through crowds and pausing all the time, for they could never anticipate when someone would catch her eye and cause her to stop. It is a tribute to those who look after her safety that they have been able to carry on with their task – and remain unobtrusive – in spite of it. The manner in which the Family behaved was much as usual: the Queen smiled politely and accepted bouquets. Philip and Charles made quips. Royals usually tend to ask the same sort of things: 'How far have you come?' 'How old are you?' 'Did you pick these yourself?' 'Do you live near here?' 'Beautiful day, isn't it?'

That these questions are often bland does not in any way make them trivial. By necessity they must be easily answered, to save the need for lengthy explanations. It is not rudeness that makes such conversations brief, but fairness. Given the demands on her time, if she spent five minutes talking to one person another half-dozen would not get to meet her, and she must therefore spread herself as thinly as possible. Contact, interaction, a few seconds of fellowship between monarch and subject, are all that is required. For those who meet the Queen is it the fact that she spoke to them, not what she said, that matters.

Her Majesty is not bored by these encounters. For one thing each occasion is different, each crowd made up of new people. For another, she enjoys the chance to see her subjects close to, and is genuinely *interested* in hearing where they have come from. Although she accepts bouquets from numerous well-wishers, she never seems burdened. After holding one for a few minutes she will discreetly pass it on to those who accompany her, and bystanders become used to the sight of a man in a suit juggling bunches of flowers. There are always at least four people following her – her Private Secretary, her Equerry, her protection officer and a lady-in-waiting. Her Majesty, like all Royals, will never give an autograph, just as the Palace will never accede to requests for a signed photograph. The Queen is not a celebrity and does not behave like one.

This is not to say that she will not oblige people in other ways, if possible. When she was still a Princess and was to visit South Wales a woman wrote to say that, on the day, she would stand in a particular spot – a hilltop at Barmouth in Merionethshire – and wave a white tablecloth. Unbeknown to her entourage, Elizabeth was looking out for her as she was driven through the town. Spotting the cloth, she stopped the car and spent several minutes talking to her. Well aware of the trouble people often take to see her, she will make herself as visible as she can.

Her appearance is always similar. Although naturally the cut and colour of her outfits will vary, the basic elements remain constant, and there is a reason for everything. The most important point is that she should be conspicuous. She must stand out in a crowd so that those who have come to see her will not be disappointed. Even if they glimpse her only as a tiny figure in the distance, they will recognise her and be able to go home feeling they have 'had their money's worth'. This is why she wears suits and dresses and hats of a uniform colour, often a pastel shade such as pink or pale yellow or orange. It was Queen Mary who began this practice of dressing in pastels, so the Queen is the third generation to do so. On occasions when she has been with other royal ladies – her mother, sister or daughter – each of them would be dressed in a different colour so that distant crowds could distinguish them. The shade of her costume may well, of course, be chosen to reflect her circumstances. If she is visiting the Irish Guards, for instance, it may be assumed that at least something she wears will be in 'St Patrick's blue', the colour of their regimental hackle.

The Queen is always formally dressed in public. She wears accoutrements – a hat and gloves – that by the 1970s were rarely still seen on ladies. Those she meets on official visits will be dressed up, and she cannot look less elegant than they do. She always wears gloves because she must shake hands with dozens if not scores of people at a time, and they are often white so that her waving hand will be visible to distant onlookers. To avoid bruising on these occasions, her hand-shake is deliberately limp and she keeps her little finger out of the way. For this reason, too, she wears no rings on her right hand. On her left she has only her wedding and engagement rings, and her gold and platinum watch, a gift from France, is always worn outside her glove on her left wrist.

Her skirts are carefully tailored to ensure that they never blow in the wind, and must allow for the fact that she is often seated on platforms above others. Her hats should not have brims so wide as to hide her face, and must not be so flimsy that a gust of wind will carry them off. The style she favoured during the 1960s and 1970s was therefore the kind of head-hugging 'helmet' shape that could be put on and forgotten. In later decades she would conspicuously favour brimmed hats with high, flat crowns, and these too make her noticeable. Her hairstyle is the result of careful planning. Until the 1960s she had a side-parting and a looser, more girlish look. By the time she reached her forties she had the swept-up, tight and tidy arrangement she has retained ever since. Inconspicuous yet familiar to the public from her portraits on banknotes, this is such a part of a national image that to change it would seem almost like redesigning the flag. For practical reasons her hair must not be liable to blow in the wind, fall in her eyes, get out of place or hide her face. Its style must also make it possible to put on a wide variety of hats, including the crown, quickly and without difficulty.

Accessories – shoes, bags, hats – are designed to be inter-changeable so that they can be worn repeatedly. Her hats, especially, can be reinvented by adding or removing bows. Her shoes are high-heeled – they give her additional height – but they must be suitable for the vast amount of standing she is obliged to do. Even her posture is therefore a matter not of natural inclination but of forethought and training. As one author commented: 'The Queen is on her feet more than the most hard-worked nurse.' She is well-practised in standing and – adopting a posture with her feet slightly apart and her weight therefore equally balanced – she can remain thus for hours without drooping, looking tired or otherwise showing the strain she must feel. Her footwear must also enable her to step over awkward things such as ship's cables and get up and down a gangplank. She carries a handbag. Early in her reign this was often of the 'clutch' variety – small and without a strap. She quickly learned that this was a liability for it permanently occupied one of her hands, and she replaced it with the type that can be hung from her arm, enabling her to accept flowers, carry an order of service or shake hands.

When she is on official business, she must be accompanied at all times by another small bag that is not noticed by the public (her lady-in-waiting usually looks after it). In it are the things she would need in an emergency – spare gloves, spare tights, barley sugar to clear her throat. Since she cannot look in the least untidy she, or her staff, must be able to undertake running repairs whenever necessary. When Prince Charles was a very small boy accompanying her by car to an engagement, he jammed a half-sucked sweet into the finger of her glove moments before she was to appear. Replacements were produced within seconds. The Queen's gloves, of which she has scores of pairs, are infinitely washable and can also be dyed, which enables them to be worn with any number of other outfits.

People often do not really notice what she is wearing, especially since her costumes can look very similar. They certainly do not appreciate the amount of planning that goes into her appearance. There is no such thing as a randomly chosen garment or an accidental ensemble. Everything she wears is the result of meticulous preparation far in advance. Even if she is receiving for 20 minutes the commanding officer of an army unit, she will have on a brooch with the regimental crest – and may then replace it with something else for her next audience. For a typical visit – and in any year there are about 30 trips to various parts of Britain, quite apart from those she makes overseas – planning starts months ahead and every item is chosen, made or cleaned. For her Jubilee in 1977, deciding on the dresses she would wear for the tours and other celebrations began in 1975. Any new garments will be fitted at the Palace, where there is a room for that purpose filled with mirrors and wardrobes, and she has never been seen in clothes that did not fit perfectly. Nor, through the attentions of a careful dresser, does she have the kind of minor accidents that may plague other women. As one author has said: 'It is a tribute to the care with which her clothes are planned that this most photo-graphed woman in the world has never been seen to hitch up a shoulder strap, tug at a hem, pat her hair, fidget with her brooch, or fuss with her hat.'

New clothes are being made for her all the time, but this does not mean she simply throws away the old ones. Quite apart from having a thrifty nature, she knows that such extrava-gance would be unacceptable to the public. Her dresses are worn often. One which she will, for instance, first have used on a state visit abroad will appear again for a regional tour in Britain, for an audience, and for an informal luncheon. The clothes she wears are, to her, largely props – accoutrements that are necessary for the performance of her official function. The wardrobe she chooses in private life is, by contrast, that of any genteel farmer's wife – tweed and wool skirts, cotton day-dresses, headscarves, clothes for riding, walking in wind and rain, handling dogs. Her garments are invariably simpler, more practical, more comfortable, and surprisingly often are off-the-peg, though they would always be altered to fit her. She wears Daks skirts, and Burberry and Barbour coats. The public is accustomed to a somewhat old-fashioned look, and expects her to be rather out-of-date. Although she sometimes wears trousers when on holiday, the thought of Her Majesty in a trouser-*suit* is hard to visualise. When she was seen briefly in just such a garment – while boarding ship for her Scottish cruise in the summer of 2010 – many were genuinely astonished.

As she passes through throngs of people in her car, she is given to waving in the posture that has long-since become famous, with her wrist elevated and her hand swivelling. It has frequently been joked that this is a mechanical arm attached to the car window. In fact, such a gesture (it was actually invented by her mother) makes perfect sense. It enables her to keep on waving for long periods without tiring her arm, which rests on the windowsill. There is no equivalent means of maintaining a smile, and only determination and practice can keep this in place. The Queen has complained that, no matter how long she smiles, someone will get a picture the instant she stops and assume that she is miserable. There are many pictures of her apparently looking glum. They are usually taken while she is in a passive situation, such as listening to a speech. Owing to the cast of her features, it so happens that when her face is in repose, the corners of her mouth turn down, suggesting bad temper when, in fact, her expression is simply neutral. If she is interested or amused, on the other hand, her smile is charming. It has to be seen, in real life and at close quarters, to be fully appreciated. There are other minor worries for someone so relentlessly in the public eye. The Queen always wears three strings of pearls. In an open vehicle in hot weather, the sun could burn her skin and leave the mark of these on her neck. She is obliged to sit holding the necklace away from her – a difficult thing when she is expected to wave as well.

In between duties, she relaxes in the manner she prefers – the *Daily Telegraph* crossword, walking the dogs, assembling jigsaws (these are often laid out on a table and she will spend a few minutes on them as she passes) and watching television. She shared with her subjects a liking for *Dad's Army*, for she,

like her mother, enjoyed this nostalgic romp with its inno-
cent humour and wartime camaraderie. She was also known
to watch regularly *Edward VII*, one of the historical epics
produced at that time, and which covered every stage of that
monarch's long life. Naturally she had a close interest in the
subject, and was greatly disappointed when, owing to some
official business or other, she missed an episode. This was, of
course, before the availability of video-recorders, but within
days the BBC had forwarded her the necessary reels so that
she could catch up.

The 1970s were years of high visibility for the Royals, whose
family celebrations offered some of the decade's few bright
moments. The Queen and Prince Philip marked their silver
wedding anniversary with a thanksgiving service in November
1972. Almost exactly a year later, in Westminster Abbey on
14 November 1973, Princess Anne became the first of their
children to marry. Visits, both domestic and overseas, by the
Queen and her relations reached a crescendo at the time of
her Silver Jubilee in 1977, and in the same year she became a
grandmother.

Princess Anne married a cavalry officer, Mark Phillips.
They were united by a passion for horses and, since this was
strong enough to leave room for little else in their lives, the
relationship was a success for a number of years. Neither
the Queen nor anyone else beyond the couple themselves
was involved in the choice. The days, it seemed, were over in
which members of Royal Houses were paired off with their
equivalents. Elizabeth's father had married a member of the
British aristocracy and the match had not been an arranged
one. She herself had similarly married for love, and might well
have chosen Philip even if he had not been a prince but a mere
naval lieutenant. That marriage was heavily encouraged, but
outside interference was limited to putting the young people
together and waiting to see if they liked each other. Her sister
had provided the real break with tradition in marrying a

professional photographer. There had been another significant change when, in 1967, the first member of the Queen's
family circle was divorced and remarried. This was her cousin,
the Earl of Harewood, who wished to marry the mother of
his son, and she at once gave permission. As Queen and head
of the House of Windsor, whose agreement (according to a
law of 1775) all its members needed in order that they marry,
Elizabeth set no conditions. From Princess Anne to her grandson William, she has approved their choice of spouse, accepting
the partners they have found through the same sort of random
circumstance that many of her subjects experience.

In March 1974 there was an attempt to kidnap Princess Anne
as she was driven along the Mall. She was with her husband,
a lady-in-waiting, a police protection officer and a chauffeur, and they were returning to the Palace late one afternoon
from a routine engagement. As their car passed the corner
of Marlborough Road, the right-hand turning for St James's
Palace, another vehicle suddenly screeched out of this side-
road and blocked their way. As their car stopped, an armed
man leapt out and ran toward them. Jim Beaton, their protection officer, got out too and put himself in front of the Princess.
He was shot three times. The gunman, Ian Ball, was overpow-
ered by several passers-by, one of whom was of that species so
disliked by the Family – a journalist. Ball had carried out this
act alone, so there was no need for a police hunt for accom-
plices. He was an unbalanced personality who had become
obsessed with mounting this operation. It transpired that he
had planned, with considerable sophistication over a period
of three years, to kidnap the Princess and hold her to ransom
for three million pounds. Beaton, who fortunately recovered –
received the George Cross. This had been an anxious moment
for all concerned, and naturally led to an extensive review of
security arrangements, but by the standards of 1970s terrorism
it could have been a great deal worse.

Despite the public spectacle their activities provided, and in spite of the schedule of duties they performed, the Family came in for an increasing amount of criticism on the grounds that they were too expensive. Prince Philip's remarks in America a few years earlier had caused horror and embarrassment at home, for he had effectively been saying that the state did not provide his family with enough to live on, and it is a strict convention that no one in an official position should criticise the government while abroad. His words also caused irritation among the British public. The 1970s were to bring serious financial hardship to many, and it seemed both insensitive and insulting that a family with such wealth and possessions should cast itself as somehow deprived.

Of course these things are relative, and by the standards of their lives and commitments the Royals were short of money. The public did not understand – until these things were subsequently explained – the distinction between their own houses (Sandringham and Balmoral) and the properties that belonged to the state (Buckingham and St James's Palaces, Windsor Castle, Holyrood). There was similarly little appreciation that the immense collections of art and antiques were not the Queen's property but were 'held in trust for the nation'. The people had not realised that 70 per cent of the Queen's Civil List income was spent paying the salaries of staff, and nor had they realised that her own domestic economies were sometimes draconian. In the 1930s her parents had had to put off the renovation of Royal Lodge because of the Depression. Now she ordered the demolition of an entire wing at Sandringham in an attempt to make the house more economical to run.

Royal finances were a subject that had not, at least in recent history, been discussed openly. Paradoxically, the British people have alternately or simultaneously-complained about the cost of the institution and expected it to be magnificent. Parliament voted to fund the monarch, as it had for centuries. The Queen and her family received annual payments through the Civil List. These payments had been fixed at the start of the reign and not increased since, and like anything else in a time of relentless inflation the sums were increasingly inadequate. The Family had other sources of income, including property, assets and investments (they have excellent financial advice!) the details of which were not vouchsafed. Although the extent of the Queen's personal wealth was not – and never has been – made public, she was frequently referred to as 'the richest woman in the world', and wild estimates of her fortune were bruited about in the press as if they were fact. The result was a Parliamentary Enquiry into the subject, or rather two enquiries, in 1971 and 1975. The first took place under Edward Heath's Conservative Government, the second under a Labour administration led by Harold Wilson. Neither man, and therefore neither party, had any desire to embarrass the monarch, but the fact remained that the Civil List income had to be brought into the light of day and investigated. One emotional issue was that of income tax, which the Queen did not pay. This situation was not a matter of course. Although George V and VI had not paid it, Edward VII and Victoria had. The Queen's exemption seemed an insult to her cash-strapped people, but both Heath and Wilson decided to continue this status, and were able to curb any more punitive inclinations among their respective back-benchers. There was no political will to change matters, and it was Parliament's decision that she remain untaxed. Parliament also concluded both enquiries by voting a substantial increase in the Civil List. Prince Philip's forthrightness had won the day.

These increases, naturally, added fuel to the flames for those who thought the monarchy an expensive luxury. The high cost of maintaining the Windsors was the theme of a book by the Scottish Communist MP Willie Hamilton, *My Queen and I*, which appeared in 1975. Hamilton, a man of extreme views, set out his arguments in moderate language (his book began with an open letter to the Queen signed 'Your wayward subject'). He was careful to make cost the basis of his attack – the issue on which he might expect most ready public agreement – and to stress that Britain could still keep its colourful military, legal and ecclesiastical ceremonial without needing a sovereign. The book sold well because of advance notoriety, but no serious politician wanted to be associated with such views – quite the reverse – and it provoked a furious reaction among monarchists. Within a short time the book was mostly forgotten, as if having a moan about the subject had cleared the air. Left-wing politicians did not want to get into a fight over the matter, with their own colleagues or the wider public, and in any case some of them even sympathised with the Family's need of a pay rise. One Labour veteran, Manny Shinwell, was quoted as saying: 'We can't have them going about in rags.'

One aspect of the decade's financial troubles was a rising tide of criticism over the visible privileges of royalty. When Princess Anne and Mark Phillips used *Britannia* on their honeymoon there was a somewhat withering reaction from press and public, although the same voices were not raised when the Queen Mother used the Royal Yacht for holiday cruises, or when the Queen herself sailed it around the Scottish coast. The public, naturally knowing little about the vessel and its use on foreign visits, thought of it as an expensive toy – a rich person's plaything that was underwritten by the taxpayer.

The public also turned its ire on the 'hangers on' in the family. Princess Margaret, who loved parties and took holidays in the Caribbean, was a sitting target. The only one of the family who lived like an international millionaire, she attracted particular resentment. Her marriage had been in difficulties for some time. She and her husband lived separate lives, and their relations were characterised by an antipathy that was deep and mutual. In 1976 she developed a close friendship with a landscape gardener, Roddy Llewellyn, who was 17 years her junior, and a doctored photograph that apparently showed them intimate and alone on a West Indian beach was published in the tabloid press. She was genuinely fond of this attentive young man, who treated her with more respect than anyone else, but this was not behaviour that public opinion could ignore when the person involved was a married woman, a mother and the recipient of public money from the Civil List. Margaret somewhat fell from grace – she had created disquiet for some time, and opinion in any case gave her some leeway because she had suffered over Townsend – but she seemed to have used up all the goodwill to which she was entitled. The public had come to see her as irresponsible and selfish. Her smoking and drinking, and the infrequency with which she smiled – as well as the perception that she did not pull her weight with official duties – added to the scandal of her private life to produce a negative image that she would never escape. She was to live the remaining quarter-century of her life somewhat in the shadows. At the height of her infamy one Labour MP called her a 'parasite'. The Queen, whose customary patience with Margaret had its limits, lamented what she called 'my sister's guttersnipe life'.

The Queen became embroiled in a constitutional crisis on the other side of the world when, in 1975, the Australian Prime Minister Gough Whitlam – the head of the elected Labour Government – was dismissed by the country's Governor-General. The latter functions on Her Majesty's behalf as a ceremonial Head of State, her on-the-spot representative, who in theory acts as a sort of referee – just as the monarch does in Britain. In a crisis of confidence in the Government, the Governor-General has the constitutional right to remove a failing Prime Minister, and this is what happened. Had Australia been a republic with a ceremonial president, that person would almost certainly have done the same thing. The matter did not involve the Queen, but she got a good deal of blame from those opposed to this move, simply because she presided over the system and the hierarchy that made it possible, and republicanism in Australia suddenly became conspicuous and vocal. It became a commonplace for journalists and pundits to predict that the monarchy would disappear, perhaps even by the Jubilee year of 1977. Although feeling ran high, and Her Majesty received sackloads of letters venting strong opinions, the furore eventually subsided. The matter was not forgotten – it remains vivid in the national consciousness to this day – but the Queen's standing survived intact. This was, however, the first time in her reign that there was a strong likelihood she would lose one of her thrones. She had not previously experienced such widespread hostility to the position she held. Her attitude was, and remains, that it is for the people of the Dominion to decide whether or not they wish her to remain. She does not canvas support – or attempt to put the case for monarchy – and more than 35 years later, despite persistent predictions that an Australian republic is imminent, she is still the country's Head of State.

As a symbol of a different kind – that of cultural link – she visited the USA in July 1976 for the country's bicentennial celebrations. She danced at a White House ball and toured Bloomingdale's store in New York, but more significantly she went to Boston, the 'Cradle of the Revolution'. In melting summer heat, she stood in front of the Old State House to make a speech in which she praised the vision and ability of America's founding fathers, and raised laughter by saying how surprised they would be to know that a descendant of George III was standing on that spot. It was indeed a significant place – the site of the infamous 1770 'Boston Massacre', in which a mob deliberately taunted British soldiers so that they could then be outraged by the retaliation. Perhaps it occurred to her that this was precisely the situation that often faced her own soldiers in Northern Ireland at that time, but her speech was conciliatory, light-hearted and well received. She was an ideal guest for the nation's 200th birthday party – a familiar and respected figure who could be relied upon to behave with dignity, to say and do the right things and to heighten the sense of occasion.

The schedule was unforgiving. For almost a week she was required to attend eight or nine events every day, beginning at around 10 a.m. and going on until midnight, with only two short breaks and two hours or so off in early evening. At a series of receptions she had to meet, greet and shake hands with over a thousand people at a time. Despite the heat and the long days she could never stifle a yawn, let her glance drift over someone's head or appear uninterested in what she was being told. She could never look anything other than perfectly groomed and permanently delighted.

After a quarter-century on the throne, Queen Elizabeth was probably the most popular, and honoured, guest anywhere. Not only was she the effective head of the English-speaking world, a symbolic figure whose presence transcended national borders and political systems, she was also the most experienced traveller and speech-maker and participant in formal events among the Heads of State. Her own conduct, as well as the minutely planned efficiency of the arrangements that surrounded her, set a benchmark for others. Her hosts were rarely unimpressed. Henry Kissinger, a veteran statesman whose praise is worth having, said that she had 'made a unique and enormous contribution to Anglo-American relations'.

She toured the Commonwealth during the 1970s. Her visits were a celebration of her Silver Jubilee, and were divided into two journeys. One was in spring, the other in autumn, not only to save her the fatigue of an entire continuous round-the-world itinerary but also to ensure that she would be home for the summer and the national celebrations there. Her travels covered an astonishing 56,000 miles altogether. They were intended to show her overseas peoples their sovereign and to reassure the Dominions that Britain – which had shifted its focus to Europe by joining the Common Market in 1973 – had not cut its links with them. Since, to a large extent, this is precisely what it *had* done, the sentimental ties of monarchy were almost all that was left to bind the former British Empire.

Whatever the reality of the situation, there was no doubting the Queen's enthusiasm for the Commonwealth, or the pleasure her visits gave.

At home, where inflation and unemployment were rampant, it was seen by the Government as inappropriate that major celebrations should mark the 25th anniversary of her accession. Although she had become Queen in February, the anniversary would be commemorated in June with a thanksgiving service at St Paul's Cathedral. The momentum for this built up slowly, because it was not known how the public would react. There had not been a Jubilee since that of George V in 1935. People did not know what it meant, how it should be celebrated or what it would involve. Nevertheless the manufacture of souvenirs began, shops started to fill with commemorative items and local organisations met to plan how their communities would mark the event. It began to look serious when Prince Charles, who had been commanding a ship, left the Navy to work full-time on coordinating the celebrations. One of his tasks was to approve the design of proposed souvenirs, a number of which were abysmal. 'He cannot believe,' said a source, 'that some of these images are supposed to represent his mother!'

In a reprise of the attitude that had been seen at the time of the Queen's wedding 30 years earlier, the Government had misread the public mood. Thinking that at a time of national austerity there was no excuse for expensive celebrations, it had not realised how much the British people wanted something to celebrate. As in 1947, so in 1977: the public turned out in droves, elated by the very fact that their recession-hit country was having a party. Her Majesty made extensive tours of Britain to ensure that the atmosphere of celebration was spread as widely as possible. Everywhere she saw bunting, flags and exuberant decorations. All over the country she was asked to unveil or open or launch things that would forever be named after her Jubilee. Municipalities dedicated parks, hospital wings, schools, sports facilities and routes for guided walks.

A chain of beacons was lit across her realm, of which she lit the first at Windsor. She was genuinely moved by the reaction of the crowds, which greeted her with undisguised joy. Regardless of the vicissitudes of the time and of people's views on the cost of maintaining the Royals, opinion polls throughout the decade had given the monarchy a solid, 75-per-cent-approval rating, and even two-thirds of young people were in favour.

The fact that she was to tour the United Kingdom meant that she was also to visit Northern Ireland. Its Protestant majority was, and is, among the monarchy's most fervent supporters, but the climate of violence in the Province was such that the Northern Ireland Secretary, Roy Mason, felt it better to cancel. The Queen – as might have been expected – overruled, telling her Private Secretary, who had raised the matter: 'Martin, we said we were going to Ulster and it would be a great pity not to.'

And so she went, greatly enhancing her popularity – though not with everyone. In the Republic, where her Jubilee was not televised, the *Irish Independent* sniffed that: 'The British queen's visit to the North is one of the most unwelcome arrangements that the inoffensive woman has ever agreed to.' Nevertheless the reception in Ulster was the most touchingly enthusiastic anywhere. As one of her chaplains put it: 'She could not believe that people had that much affection for her.'

The Jubilee itself was celebrated on 7 June 1977. A grey, overcast day that brightened in the afternoon, it was not the test of endurance that the Coronation had been. People slept in the streets all along the processional route from the Palace to St Paul's, and cheered the golden coach just as they had a quarter-century earlier. As always, the splendour of uniforms, liveries, horse-furniture and brass instruments made the event a visual banquet. The Queen dressed in pink and wore one of the turban hats that were a trademark at that time, Prince Philip was in the uniform of an Admiral of the Fleet, and Prince Charles wore that of Colonel of the Welsh Guards.

The Cathedral service, attended by the entire Family and a vast assemblage of the great and good, was followed by lunch at Guildhall, after which they returned to the Palace and appeared on the balcony.

For millions of her subjects the day was one of local celebration. In countless photo albums there are pictures of long-haired men, and adults and children in flared trousers – that somehow look more dated than the Tudor costume of the Beefeaters – eating sausages at village fêtes, running in egg-and-spoon races, waving from floats or tangled in maypoles. Both Queen and country seemed blessed. A British player, Virginia Wade, won Wimbledon that year. The Queen's horse, Dunfermline, won both the Pretty Polly Stakes and the St Leger. The Jubilee was the biggest party for a generation and resoundingly demonstrated the monarchy's ability to make people feel better about themselves. It had happened just in time, for an astrologer had predicted that the Queen would abdicate on the 25th anniversary of her Coronation – in 1978.

Once the celebrations were over, reality returned. Two years afterwards, as the country was enjoying the sunshine of an August Bank Holiday weekend, news came that Lord Mountbatten had been murdered while on holiday in the west of Ireland. He had regularly spent his summers there and was known, and loved, by local people. He had disregarded the danger of terrorist attack, feeling that he was too old to be a target and that his well-known (and surprising, given his snobbery) left-wing views would also offer some protection. He was blown up by a bomb placed on a small fishing boat in which he was leaving harbour. The explosion killed him, as well as one of his twin grandsons, his son-in-law's mother and a local boy. Unusually the Queen and Prince Philip were not at Balmoral (as they would be on another August Bank Holiday when death touched the Family) but on a private tour of the Loire chateaux in France. They returned at once, and Mountbatten received a state funeral in London. The last image of the decade for Royalty was that of a coffin drawn on a gun-carriage by sailors processing through the streets and the Family, grief-stricken but as stoical as always, bidding farewells.

# REVIVAL, 1980–1990

'I meet so many mad people . . .'

Trooping the Colour. The Mall lined with Union Flags, hanging limp. The crowds, happy in the June sunshine behind the crush-barriers, applauding politely rather than cheering. The red tarmac roadway recently swept, but littered with droppings from the horses that had already passed that way. The policemen stationed at intervals, the sunlight glinting on their silver helmet-plates. The Guardsmen, also precise widths apart. The ones on the left, unlucky to be on the north side and thus having the sun in their eyes, perhaps squinting under the fringes of black bearskin. A husky, aristocratic voice shouting the order: 'Royal Salute! Pree-sent . . . Arms!' and the three precise, staccato crashes of hand on rifle-stock as they did so. The officers' swords dipping in salute. The clatter of a police chopper overhead. The flash of cameras from the shadowed gloom under the trees. The distant blare of band-music and the thump-thump-thump of a big drum, drifting across the Park.

The Queen loved this occasion. She had known it all her life, and had presided over it many times. She admired the discipline, smartness, perfection with which the Guards regiments went through this solemn and magnificent ceremony, for they showed the same desire to be precise in every detail that characterised her own nature. She was immensely proud that these soldiers, the finest in the world, were *hers*, and she wondered what the onlookers were thinking as they watched them pass. Those that were her subjects would share her pride. Those that were not would feel envy, and perhaps a touch of awe. While her husband – who was at her right shoulder – naturally favoured the Navy, she had always preferred the Army. She had an Inspector General's eye for uniforms and a Sergeant Major's knowledge of drill. She was now in the uniform of the Welsh Guards, whose Colour was to be trooped that day.

She loved the horses, too: the huge Cavalry Blacks of the Life Guards and the Blues and Royals, the light draught horses of the King's Troop, the placid, lumbering piebald drumhorses that were so popular with the crowds. She herself had recruited one of these. While in Edinburgh she had spotted him, pulling a cart. Now this horse, Cicero, carried a pair of great silver kettledrums, and was much too grand to want reminding of his humble origins.

Her own horse, a mare called Burmese, had been a gift from the Royal Canadian Mounted Police, and had served with her at this event since 1969. She was as quiet and disciplined as any of the military mounts on parade that day. She moved at a steady pace. There was no hurry. The distance between the Palace forecourt and Horse Guards' arch had been measured to the second, so that the Queen would reach it precisely as the clock overhead was striking 11. The crowd in the stands would rise in their seats, the troops would present arms, the national anthem would be played in that slow, languid tempo, and the Royal Standard would be broken from the roof of the building just as her horse came to a halt.

She was almost at the Admiralty Citadel, where the procession turns right into Approach Road and the parade ground, when there were sudden noises on the right. Shots. Someone was firing shots.

There was a communal gasp. Police spun round, scanning the faces behind the barriers. Heads ducked instinctively throughout the crowd, but when people looked up the Queen was still sitting on her horse in the same straight-backed posture.

On duty at that corner was Lance Corporal Galloway of 2nd Battalion, Scots Guards. Like other 'street liners', his function was to present arms as Her Majesty went by. He was about seven yards from her when, as he later recalled in the laconic language of a military report: 'There was a noise which I thought was the crowd clapping; then I recognised it was gunfire. I turned round and saw a man pointing a gun at the Queen, and as I turned he fired the last shot. The crowd was shouting and he was being pushed forward. I leaned across the barrier, grabbed him by the hair and pulled him into the Mall [where police took hold of him. Then] I returned to my position.'

Onlookers saw the Queen pat her horse's neck in a calming gesture. Her Majesty later said that the animal had become nervous not because of the shots but owing to the sudden activity as other riders closed in protectively around her. The procession moved onto the parade ground as if nothing were amiss, though the waiting audience had heard the noise and was straining to see. The television commentator paused only for seconds, briefly announced that shots seemed to have been fired at the Queen, and resumed. The ceremony went ahead entirely as usual, and she rode back along the Mall when it was over.

In terms of coolness in adversity, that day in June 1981 was Her Majesty's finest hour – a tribute not only to her personal courage but to the training she had received. The man responsible, one of those disturbed and attention-seeking youths who seem so often to be behind such acts, had been armed only with a starting pistol, which he fired six times. The Queen had not been in danger, though naturally no one could have known that. The perpetrator, Marcus Sarjeant, had sought to become 'the most famous teenager in the world' through this act. He would have used a real weapon and live bullets had he been able to obtain them. Sentenced to five years in jail, he was to write to the Queen to apologise. He received no reply.

It had already been a dangerous year for world leaders. In March, another disturbed young man had attempted to shoot Ronald Reagan in Washington. Although the President was hit only by ricochet, the bullet passed within an inch of his heart. In May, Pope John Paul II had been hit four times by a would-be assassin's bullets in St Peter's Square. His attacker, a Turk called Mehmet Ali Ajca, had originally decided to shoot the British monarch but, on learning that this was a woman, had sought another victim. In the same month a bomb had exploded in the normally peaceful Shetland Islands while the Queen was opening the new oil terminal at Sullom Voe. The device was small, and it damaged only a boiler in a part of the premises Her Majesty was not visiting. Nevertheless this was seen as an assassination attempt, and these were fraught times for those charged with Royal protection. As a result of the incident in the Mall, police were ordered on all future occasions to face into the crowd, not away from it, and those sitting in the stands for the ceremony were subjected to searches.

This had been the first notable occurrence in a decade that would bring mixed fortunes to Britain and its Royal Family. The events that defined it almost all took place in its first half: the Falklands campaign – a short and distant, but full-scale war, in which her second son took part; the race riots in British cities and the interminable miners' strike of 1984, a nasty showdown between the trade unions and a government that sought to break their power. As in the 1970s, the news images that filled television screens were often ugly and disturbing – pickets, riots and burning buildings – but this time there were also burning warships, hit by Exocet missiles. Terrorism continued to be a plague – one bomb went off within earshot of the Queen and killed members of her Household Cavalry. These were grim years, but at least the country was seeing a return to prosperity.

Once again, it was the House of Windsor that provided the brighter moments, the excuse to celebrate. The Queen's two eldest sons were married in ceremonies that were watched by television audiences throughout the world, and the women they brought into the Family changed public perceptions of royalty for a generation. There were Royal grandchildren at frequent intervals: Zara (1981), William (1982), Harry (1984) and Beatrice (1988). The Royal Family now had more members than at any time since the reign of Victoria. Such interest was generated by these events that two new magazines, *Royalty* and *Majesty*, began publication.

During these years, as during the decade that followed, the Queen's life would largely be defined by the activities of her children. It was the 1980s that became a watershed between an old-style monarchy and a new. The change was to cost it a good deal of dignity.

The focus for a great amount of public sentiment was Charles's wedding to Lady Diana Spencer in July 1981. The Prince had reached the age of 32 without marrying and there was a certain impatience both within his family and in the public at large. His father, who had married at 26, told him pointedly that unless he made a decision soon there would be no suitable brides left. Charles had always been of an indecisive nature, but he was also happy with the informal friendships he already had, one of which was with the married Camilla Parker Bowles. Both his parents wanted not only to see him settled but also to have the succession secured.

The Prince had had no shortage of girlfriends, most of them from upper-class English backgrounds, many of them seemingly suitable in temperament. One of these, Lady Sarah Spencer, had a younger sister whom Charles met at a shoot on her family's estate. Even as a teenager, Diana projected considerable charm, humour and personality. She was athletic, tomboyish, affectionate and possessed a winsome beauty that had not yet quite blossomed. Her family was well-versed in the ways of the Court (her grandmother was a close friend of Charles's grandmother) and she had lived for some years on the Sandringham Estate, thus enabling the press to suggest that she was 'the girl next door'. She was sufficiently young not to have a 'past'. She was not academic – her school record was lamentable – but she had less quantifiable attributes of grace and empathy that promised well. For months during the winter of 1980–1981, speculation mounted that the 19-year-old was going to marry Charles. She was besieged by the media – followed in the street by press photographers – and she endured the attention with seeming patience and good humour. Her trademark shyness, her habit of keeping her head demurely lowered, peering at the world through falling blond locks, made her an instant icon.

In theory, Diana was a highly suitable future queen. She came from the landed aristocracy whose world was so familiar to Her Majesty. She appeared to enjoy the same country pursuits. Her appealing modesty and her patent affection for children suggested that she would win the nation's affection with ease (she did) and slip comfortably into a life of public duty (she didn't), but even before she was married a different personality was becoming evident.

Charles proposed during a dinner, and allowed her to consider her answer for some weeks while she made a trip to Australia. Their engagement was announced after her return, on 24 February 1981, when a series of pictures was taken of the couple in the Palace gardens. At five feet 11 inches – the same height as her fiancé – she seemed doomed to wear flat shoes for the rest of her life, but this seemed the extent of her problems. 'With Prince Charles by my side, I cannot go wrong,' she was quoted as saying. The wedding date was set for 29 July 1981, and a public holiday was declared. Souvenir-manufacturers rubbed their hands. The nation got ready to celebrate. The preparations were so ubiquitous and the general sense of mounting excitement so great that they threatened to produce a sense of overkill, and T-shirts were sold with the legend 'What Wedding?' printed on them. The Queen was both happy and relieved. A spouse had been found for her son who appeared entirely suitable, and of whom both the Family and the Commonwealth were fond. Diana seemed to 'tick every box'.

Yet with the engagement a powerful new element was to enter the House of Windsor, and the Queen may well have been somewhat irked at the attention this new member received from the press, for she herself was now overtaken in media attention by her daughter-in-law.

The wedding was as glorious an occasion as it had promised to be. Held at St Paul's – Prince Charles's choice of setting – it was a magnificent set-piece of music, architecture and costume. Vestments and uniforms dazzled, trumpets and choir, organ and soloists sent collective goose bumps through the congregation. The groom was in the dress uniform of a senior naval officer, the bride – on whom the watching millions focused their attention – wore a dress of white silk taffeta with a train 25 feet long. It was not seen until she emerged from her coach at the cathedral steps and, as she walked up the long aisle (a journey that took three-and-a-half minutes) it was shown to greatest advantage on television screens by cameras looking down from the gallery. Viewers noticed how much Prince Philip and the Queen were smiling throughout. The day's most memorable moment occurred later when, on the Palace balcony, the bride and groom kissed in front of cheering crowds.

The service was the most popular Royal event since the Coronation. Some 600,000 people waited in the streets to see the procession, and 3,500 were in the Cathedral. A truly staggering number – 750 million – watched it on television throughout the world. This audience included a Soviet warship anchored just outside British territorial waters. It was also reported that one man, who had taken a ferry to France to escape all the fuss, was furious when the vessel's crew stopped engines in mid-Channel and settled down to watch.

However, Charles and Diana were not, by any stretch of the imagination, a well-matched couple. The gap in their ages was much greater than the 12 years that separated them. He had always been old for his age, and the women whose company he most enjoyed tended to be mature and somewhat maternal. A product of the 1950s and 1960s, there had never been a time when he embraced the culture of youth that was then sweeping away everything in its path. He has never cared for rock music and has never dressed like a member of his age group. Never attracted to the passing fads of his own generation, he was unlikely to feel any empathy with hers. His traditional nature gave him a gravitas for which many are thankful, and which suits him well for the position he holds, but it meant that he and Diana seemed more like a middle-aged father and his teenage daughter than husband and wife. She did not share his love of opera and high culture, nor did she like his friends, who were of his age group or even older and who – by definition – shared his conservative tastes. There was absolutely no meeting of minds or pleasure in serious discussion, which for Charles was very important. She demanded a level of attention that he was not accustomed to giving anyone, and she became strident, moody and argumentative. Obsessed with the notion that Camilla Parker Bowles was still part of his life, she became possessive. Like his mother, Charles hated confrontation and preferred to wish problems away. Diana favoured having things out and goading him into a response. He could not relate to someone whose level of cultural awareness was so far below his own, and he greatly resented the fact that his own personality and achievements were nudged aside by a media that was interested only in his wife's wardrobe and hairstyles.

Diana was horrified at what she saw as the cold formality of her husband's family. No one, she complained, gave her the guidance necessary to fulfil her role. She was expected to accustom to a world of state banquets, speech-making, inspection of troops and participating in walkabouts, without anyone – including her husband, to whom all this was second nature – showing her properly how it was done. All this was understandably intimidating for a nursery-school assistant, even one with an aristocratic background. Her frustration often vented itself in rage.

Her criticism was unfair. Charles was often touchingly concerned about the pressure to which she was subjected. Courtiers were on hand to explain what was necessary (she saw them instead as always telling her what to do). Her parents-in-law, under no illusions that life would be difficult, stood ready to help her should she ask, though effective communications were somehow never established between them. Help was not consistently given – all those around her were busy – and she was expected to learn more quickly than she perhaps felt was reasonable.

Diana had, before her marriage, naturally been used to all the freedoms of a well-off young woman in London. She simply could not accustom to the restrictions of living within the Household – having her life planned for months or even years in advance, being expected to be on duty when she did not feel like it, being accompanied everywhere by a protection officer. Having a more impulsive nature than the members of her husband's family could ever have afforded, she felt trapped.

At the end of that year the Princess, who found it increasingly hard no longer to be able to run ordinary errands, was photographed going from her home at Highgrove to buy sweets. She was sufficiently upset by this unrelenting attention for the Queen to call a conference of newspaper editors and request a gentler approach. She was persuasive and reasonable, but when asked by the editor of the *News of the World* why the Princess could not 'send a servant to buy her Fruit Gums', Her Majesty retorted: 'That's the most pompous thing I have ever heard.' Perhaps so, but it highlighted an important problem – that it was not possible to have privacy and celebrity at the same time.

The very notion of 'celebrity' is not what the Royal Family is about. Many people confuse being in the public eye with being famous, exciting and glamorous. Diana was quickly described as having 'star quality', as if she were a Hollywood actress, and this concept will probably have irritated the Queen. It is not the purpose of Royalty to entertain or to provide fashion tips. Her family's function is to be constant, dutiful and, if necessary, dull. Their mission is to set a quiet example, to reflect the lives of her subjects, not that of the international rich. Royals need no publicity, they do not draw attention to themselves, their clothes, their lifestyle. They are just there, doing their job regardless of changing fashion. They do not want to be associated with the self-promoting, tinsel world of the cinema or the weather-cock nature of changing fashion. With Diana, the press decided she was both a celebrity and a Royal. The distinction became blurred, and traditionalists were horrified by the tide of media attention that resulted. Diana undoubtedly won friends for the monarchy in her early years, but the image she represented was not the one the Queen believed was right.

The cracks in her marriage did not appear at once, and for several years the Family enjoyed a level of positive press interest that was tantamount to a honeymoon. Since her engagement she had had something of a makeover. With advice and assistance from the fashion press and from stylists, her clothing, hair and make-up became steadily more sophisticated, replacing the artless, schoolgirlish look that the public had found so endearing. With her statuesque build, photogenic features and the high exposure of her position, she had everything necessary to be a fashion leader. That she also smiled readily, had a nice sense of humour and a genuine way with people (she spoke to strangers with more spontaneous warmth than the other Royals) made her yet more popular. When in March 1983 she and her husband visited Australia, they took with them the nine-month-old Prince William. It was a joint decision – though Diana got the credit – and proved immensely popular with Australians. It was believed, erroneously, that she had brought him against the Queen's wishes. Nevertheless, the days when Royal infants were left at home while their parents went on official tours were clearly over. This change was seen as evidence that Diana had brought a greater humanity to the House of Windsor.

Yet whatever she brought in terms of popular appeal, it had become apparent that Diana would not fit easily into the routine of the Family. The young woman who had looked so shy in photographs proved to be stubborn and wilful. She admired the Queen enormously and said so often. She was impressed by the monarch's stamina and unflagging devotion to duty, but she did not want to emulate it. She committed numerous small gaffes – or deliberate floutings of etiquette – arriving late for meals, deciding to go to bed in the midst of an evening when guests were present, and using ill-health and, especially, headaches (that catch-all excuse for avoiding anything unpleasant) to get out of official duties. Although she was both loyal and enthusiastic regarding the charities she took up, she never learned the lesson that Royalty cannot do things – or cancel things – on impulse. The Queen, to whom illness was simply weakness and who had never been seriously unwell, had little sympathy with Diana's protestations. When, in November 1984, Diana attended the State Opening of Parliament, she famously sported a new, swept-up hairstyle, designed to set off the tiara she wore. This received massive newspaper coverage and diverted attention completely from the Queen's speech. Her Majesty was clearly deeply irritated. She was to refer to her daughter-in-law as 'that impossible girl'.

But there had been other preoccupations. In April 1982, Argentine forces suddenly seized the Falkland Islands, a British dependency in the South Atlantic to which they had long laid claim. The government in Buenos Aires, attempting to divert attention from a surging economic crisis, expected a cheap victory because a nation 8,000 miles away would not – or could not – fight to recapture them. They had seriously underestimated the Prime Minister, Margaret Thatcher, who came into her own in this crisis. Without hesitation the British Government assembled a task force and sent it, in whatever vessels could be scraped together, to the rescue of the islanders. While America tried to settle the dispute peacefully through exhaustive shuttle diplomacy, the toughest members of the British Armed forces – marines, paratroops, ghurkas – made the long voyage southward. Also in the task force was Prince Andrew, the Queen's favourite child. A Sub-Lieutenant aboard HMS *Invincible*, he had recently qualified as a pilot on Sea King helicopters. Although his skills were needed in the conflict, the Ministry of Defence had wished to shunt him out of danger into some administrative job. It was the Queen who insisted he take the same risks as his comrades, and so he went. Yet again, she drew on personal courage.

The campaign (neither side ever actually declared war) lasted for 74 days. It cost the lives of 257 British personnel and more than twice that number of Argentines, as well as three local people. There were moments of tragedy, horror and triumph, and there was considerable heroism among men fighting in difficult terrain and conditions. Andrew fulfilled the tasks he was set: anti-submarine patrols, evacuating casualties and – not without danger – acting as a decoy for Exocets. His mother, like that of other servicemen, avidly and apprehensively watched the television news each day. Since this was heavily censored and gave little real information, she also gleaned all she could from the other sources at her disposal – the Ministry of Defence, the Admiralty and Downing Street.

Once the war ended, on 14 June 1982, she was able to speak to him by telephone in the capital, Port Stanley, and asked him to convey her pride and gratitude to all of those there. When the task force arrived back in Portsmouth, the Queen and Prince Philip were waiting, as were thousands of others, to greet them. In this conflict it had been Mrs Thatcher who played the role of Elizabeth at Tilbury, but Elizabeth II had expressed her people's anxiety and pride. Her son had been the first of the born-Royal family members to take part in action since her father had been at Jutland in 1916. One wonders how she – and the nation – would have reacted had he been lost.

Just after 7:15 on the morning of 9 July 1982, Her Majesty awoke at the Palace to find a strange man in her bedroom, drawing the curtains. He sat on her bed. Agitated and rambling, he was barefoot and wore jeans. His right hand was dripping blood onto the counterpane and he held a broken glass ashtray. He spoke to her about his personal problems, which involved complex family relationships. The Queen kept him talking, but pressed a bell that connected with the police control room. Nothing happened. She tried another that linked with the corridor outside. Again, there was no response.

She was not normally alone. Her husband, with official duties that day, had slept elsewhere so as not to disturb her when setting off early. A policeman guarded her bedroom every night, wearing slippers so that his footsteps would not disturb her, but he had gone off duty at six o'clock as usual. At that time he was replaced by a footman, who was at that moment walking the corgis in the gardens. A maid who might have heard the bell was cleaning in a nearby room with the door closed. When the man asked for a cigarette, the Queen seized the opportunity by telling him she had none but could find some. Opening the door into the corridor she encountered the maid, who famously exclaimed: 'Bloody hell, Ma'am! What's he doing here?' Just then the Page returned and, keeping the visitor calm with promises to find him a drink, led him through a door and grabbed hold of him. The police arrived, about 10 minutes after the first of the Queen's calls. As an officer appeared in the corridor, Her Majesty shouted 'Get in there!' and the man was apprehended.

The kidnap attempt on Princess Anne, the shots in the Mall and now this. The Royal Family has been fortunate that, given the scale of international terrorism in recent years, the occasions on which their personal safety has been most compromised have all involved not sophisticated or fanatical political operatives but solitary obsessives who have either not sought to kill or have lacked the means to do so. This one was the least harmful of them. Michael Fagan was an unemployed, 31-year-old schizophrenic. He had, it transpired, visited the Palace before, climbing through an open window and taking a bottle of wine. On this occasion, he had got over the garden wall and in through a window that proved to contain George V's stamp collection. Unable to open a locked door into the corridor, he had exited through the window and, climbing a drainpipe, entered another – ironically, finding himself in the office of the man responsible for the Queen's security. He wandered along a corridor, having acquired the ashtray, which he broke. He passed a housekeeper and greeted her, and he found his way to Her Majesty's bedroom (which has a name-card on the door). He had apparently thought of committing suicide there, slashing his wrists with the glass, but decided that after all this 'wasn't a nice thing to do'. His mother later said that he was a great admirer of the Queen and had probably just wanted to tell her his troubles.

The public was outraged. The Prime Minister apologised for the lapse of vigilance. Several police officers were abruptly removed from the Palace. It was discovered that Fagan had been seen entering the grounds by an off-duty officer who had reported him, but that he could not be found when a search was made. It was also learned that the alarm the Queen had twice pressed was not taken seriously because it tended to go off by accident. 'It's that bloody bell again!' said the man on duty in the control room – switching it off for the second time.

Her Majesty was much admired for her handling of the situation. She had experienced every woman's nightmare, and had had no idea if Fagan was armed or determined to harm her. Yet she made light of the experience, quipping: 'Well, I meet so many mad people that it didn't surprise me so much.' Once Fagan had been taken away, she apparently returned to bed and drank her morning tea. She had wanted no word of the incident to be made public, but the press found out and it became one of the major news stories of the year. A very considerable review of security, needless to say, followed. Apart from anything else, the officer outside the Queen's door at night was now armed.

Protection of the Royal Family has to be unobtrusive. In the USA, the presence around the President of large men with sunglasses and bulging jackets is seen as a useful deterrent to evil-doers. The Royal Family prefer discretion, and wish to look as ordinary as possible. Protection officers dress according to their surroundings – wearing tailcoats at Ascot, for example – and are remarkably difficult to identify or to distinguish from the other men who surround the sovereign. Individual members of the Family, both past and present, have hated the sight of uniformed officers in their vicinity and have wanted their police attendants to be invisible.

For the whole of the 1980s, and for the first time, her Prime Minister was a woman. Some in the media had predicted that the two ladies would enjoy a warm rapport, for they were not only the same gender but also the same age. Once the working relationship had begun, however, it was widely rumoured that the atmosphere was frigid, even hostile. The truth is somewhere in between. Because their dealings lasted more than 10 years, there will naturally have been ups and downs, moments of agreement and empathy as well as aloofness and irritation. It is unarguable that they were entirely different personalities, and had very little in common (though the Queen Mother, whose opinions carried great weight with her daughter, thoroughly approved of Mrs Thatcher). Like her predecessor, Edward Heath, the Prime Minister had no liking for small talk. She was not interested in racing or country pursuits, and did not enjoy visits to Balmoral. She also had a commanding manner, which, while it had made her an effective party leader, could tend to seem like lecturing when she explained policy at weekly audiences. The Prime Minister's gender will not have been helpful, for the Queen happens to prefer dealing with men – her senior advisors have all been – and she does not like having to share the stage with other high-profile females. Nevertheless, Mrs Thatcher was a devout monarchist and admired the Queen's sense of duty. Her Majesty has always been punctilious in respecting the choice of the electorate. Each was therefore inclined toward willingness to cooperate, no matter what their personal feelings may have been.

Relations, however, depended to a large extent on the shifting circumstances of a very stormy decade. It is likely that the Queen approved of Mrs Thatcher's stand over the Falklands, while the nadir was perhaps reached in 1983 when American forces invaded Grenada – part of the British Commonwealth – without informing London. The Queen was reported to be incandescent, and demanded to see Mrs Thatcher at once to discuss the situation. So insistent was she that the Prime Minister was obliged to leave halfway through an emergency Cabinet meeting on the matter to go to the Palace.

There were other causes of friction. Mrs Thatcher's refusal to support sanctions against the apartheid regime in South Africa was a massive disruption at the 1985 Commonwealth Heads of Government Conference, over which the Queen presided. The British Prime Minister's unyielding opposition to the use of such measures, in the face of overwhelming contrary opinion, caused such ill-feeling that it threatened to destroy – by provoking widespread boycotts – the Commonwealth Games in 1986. The Queen, whose commitment to good race relations was unimpeachable, was at best anguished and at worst furious.

It was reported, in a *Sunday Times* article in 1986, that Her Majesty was horrified by the Prime Minister's authoritarian personal style and her confrontational approach to industrial relations, that her methods were 'divisive' and that she 'lacked compassion', especially towards the less privileged. This was speculation, even though the source of information was believed to be the Palace Press Office. It is safe to say that the Queen was indeed horrified by strikes and riots during those years – who would not have been? – and that she deplored any threat to the stability of her realm, but it can also be said with certainty that she would never have expressed views on the governance of the country that could have been heard by anyone, let alone communicated to the press. To do so would have been a breach of her carefully maintained political neutrality, and to leak such notions to the media would surely have cost someone in her Press Office their job.

The perception of hostility between monarch and Prime Minister was heightened considerably by a Channel 4 programme broadcast in 2009. Part of a series on the Queen, it dramatised the relationship with a good deal of invented dialogue (Prince Philip sneers at 'That bloody grocer's daughter', while Her Majesty crows that 'I actually managed to get a word in edgeways!' at a weekly audience). Between scenes, there were interviews with political figures whose memories seemed to support the thesis. It is worth remembering that even if the quoted outbursts were true, it is not unlikely that the Queen – in the heat of the moment and the privacy of her home – might say such things, without these being taken as permanent views or official pronouncements. It is also worth remembering that Her Majesty was to attend Mrs Thatcher's

70th birthday party, and that she would make her a Baroness – an honour that, according to the Palace, 'would not have been given without the utmost respect for the recipient'.

On 23 July 1986, the second royal wedding of the decade took place. Prince Andrew, a career naval officer, married Sarah Ferguson, a young woman he had known as a child. She was the second daughter of a former Household Cavalry major who was polo manager to Prince Charles. She was also a friend of Princess Diana, whom she had met when she was 14. Diana, feeling out of place in the Family, saw the benefits of bringing in this lively and compatible girl as an ally, and was active in putting her in Andrew's way, though Sarah was vivacious enough to catch his eye in any case. The couple sat together at lunch at a Windsor house party during Ascot Week in 1985. Flame-haired and boisterous, Sarah was patently good company for him. They shared a somewhat knockabout sense of humour, and mutual attraction was swift. Their engagement was announced the following March. This couple were entirely unlike the Waleses. There was no gap in years. Both were the same age, with Sarah a few months older, and there was no danger of introspection – or high cultural awareness – on the part of either.

This time the wedding was at Westminster Abbey. As befitted a more modest event, things were on a smaller scale: the television audience was 500 million and the bride – who arrived in the Glass Coach just as Diana had done – had a 17-foot-long train. Shortly before the ceremony, the groom was created Duke of York, a title traditionally given to second sons and last held by the Queen's father. At the ceremony, Sarah looked splendid – even if there were unkind mutterings about her weight – and she pleased traditionalists by promising in her vows to 'obey' her husband, not least because this was a phrase Diana had omitted. She was popular with the public, which had taken to using her nickname, 'Fergie', and which saw her as a no-nonsense, sensible country girl whose sense of fun would save her from being infected by the stuffiness of the Court. The Queen liked her, too. They often rode together at Windsor (the Yorks lived at nearby Sunningdale), and Her Majesty sometimes referred to her as 'my daughter'.

Yet Sarah somehow could not do anything right. Remarkably quickly she was being sniped at in the press for being too large, too noisy, too free-spending, too undignified. At Ascot in 1987, photographers captured a moment of juvenile horseplay – Sarah and Diana poking, with their umbrellas, the behind of another young woman. The newspapers reacted with annoyance, calling them 'silly, simpering girls' and accusing them of 'fooling about in a most childish manner', and this image stuck. The Duchess also became infamous for the number of expense-paid holidays she took, as well as for the fact that when her first child was born she did not even come up with a name for the girl for several weeks. For her part, Sarah found herself bored because her husband was at sea for lengthy periods and, like Diana, she found the constant expectations that went with royal status irksome and constricting. She was to admit, years later, that 'I didn't understand the rules', but she seemed to make little attempt to learn them. Another later comment – 'I was never cut out for Royalty' – was one with which few would disagree.

The creeping notion of monarchy as 'just like the rest of us' was seen to embarrassing effect in the case of Prince Edward. With Gordonstoun and a spell in New Zealand under his belt, he wished to attend Cambridge University. In past generations some of his forebears, including his grandfather, had done so (Edward VII, when Prince of Wales, was sent to Oxford as well – so as not to show favouritism), while his great uncle, later Edward VIII, was at Oxford. It was a mere formality to enrol, and the university was honoured to have them, though they tended to be kept apart from other undergraduates and tutored privately. Prince Charles – the first Royal to go to school, and whose parents had wanted him to be treated the same as any other pupil – had passed into Trinity despite having results that were modest by Cambridge standards. Half a generation later, Edward only just got away with the same trick. His enrolment at Jesus College provoked a protest from other students and objections from the faculty. He was pilloried in the satirical press, even though his tutor was subsequently to say that his mind was impressive. It was obvious that the notion of Royalty automatically helping themselves to the best of everything would no longer be accepted by public opinion, and the mistake was not made in the case of Prince Charles's sons, or any of the younger Royals. It was clear that they would now have to work for, and earn, the respect that used to be automatic.

Edward's troubles were not over. He had been sponsored through Cambridge by the Royal Marines, in which he had enlisted as an officer, with a commitment – after graduation – to undertake its famously exacting training course. His interests by that time had crystallised, and led him in other directions. Joining in the summer of 1986, he initially did well in training, but his doubts increased and he decided that he would 'wrap', to use the Corps term for requesting discharge. Apart from earning his father's fury, he faced the prospect of having to repay the cost of his university education. His decision to abandon the course took a great deal of courage, considering the humiliation that was heaped upon him and which he had known was coming. The standards involved were extremely high and beyond the reach of most people. Merely trying was commendable and to fail was no shame whatever, and his reason for going was a change of mind rather than a failure to meet demands, but because people *expect* Royalty to have an inside edge – expert guidance, endless practice, all manner of behind-the-scenes assistance – for them seemingly to flounder in open competition suggests inadequacy indeed. The notion that they would compete on equal terms with their subjects in classrooms, playing fields and assault courses was one that appealed to the spirit of an egalitarian age. Sometimes it worked, as when Princess Anne gained success in equestrian events and competed in the Olympics. When there were mistakes, misfortunes or outright failures, however, the monarchy found itself vulnerable to ridicule. Just as bad, for them, was the notion that if they did succeed at something it could be attributed to some bending of the rules.

As members of the Family – the younger generation, at least – became more accessible through interviews, the public came to see them as increasingly ordinary. Edward continued to court derision by taking a job as a production assistant with Andrew Lloyd-Webber's Really Useful Theatre Company, despite the fact that he was working for a living and experiencing a closer brush with 'ordinary life' than anyone in his family had known. He naturally wanted to progress to staging his own productions, and an attempt was made with the screening of *It's a Royal Knockout*, a charity fundraising event organised by the Prince and involving his brother Andrew and sister-in-law Sarah as well as Princess Anne. It was modelled on a highly popular television programme, but stuffed with celebrities in a manner that is now commonplace. The event was intended to be slapstick; it raised money for good causes and it was not the Royals – who, in period dress, were team captains – that had to look and behave idiotically, running about and falling over. Nevertheless it was seen as undignified, the press did not like it and the Prince made no friends when he lost his temper with them afterwards. The endless replaying on television of the moment he stalked out of the press conference is a particular cruelty to a young man who had meant well and whose only crime had been a certain cockiness. In a family that lives constantly under scrutiny, youthful errors of judgement simply do not go away.

Only Princess Anne's conduct seemed to give complete satisfaction. She was created Princess Royal by the Queen in 1987 to acknowledge her work for charity. Whatever the problems caused or endured by her children, Her Majesty remained officially silent. She had disapproved of her son's television programme, but made no public comment. Lord Mountbatten had admired the calm with which she weathered such squalls, once remarking that: 'Most people can hide their family difficulties, but hers are always the focus of public attention.' Where her children are concerned she will, in any case, hear no criticism.

For them, and by extension for her, this was a painful transitional period between the privileged past and the meritocratic future.

# HORRIBILIS, 1990–2000

'This is not a year on which I will look back
with undiluted pleasure.'

In 1992 the BBC released a documentary called *Elizabeth R*.
In the year that commemorated the 40th anniversary of her
accession, it was thought worthwhile to remind the public
what Her Majesty did. This happens periodically. Because so
much of her work goes on out of sight, or is too routine to
merit mention, it is through this sort of vehicle with its 'fly
on the wall' or 'year in the life' approach that both a national
and an international audience can see how hard she works,
how varied is the round of duties she performs and – through
glimpses of her when off duty – how attractive her personality is in private. The footage had been filmed during 1990 and
1991. Viewers watched her hosting a visit by the President of
Poland, chatting easily with the Prime Minister at Balmoral,
welcoming troops home from the first Gulf War, touring parts
of the United Kingdom, and – a note of mild farce – speaking
on the White House lawn into a microphone that had not been
adjusted after the much-taller President Bush had welcomed

her. Only her hat and glasses were visible. She retrieved the situation when later she addressed another audience – the US Congress – by opening with the words: 'I hope you can all see me today.'

The programme was a great success. It was notable for the mirth, the banter and the sense of fun that the Queen displayed. She looked delighted to be doing her job. There was a sense of enjoyment, of pleasure and light-heartedness at going through the pre-arranged and formal functions that filled her days. She also showed a genuine curiosity about those who came to the Palace, a desire to meet people whose achievements had brought them to her notice – while awaiting one visitor, she rubbed her hands with excited glee. She laughed out loud at jokes or at mild mishaps that befell those around her. She seemed to smile more often in the course of this single programme than in four decades of public appearances.

Perhaps the most revealing glimpse was of Her Majesty attending the 1991 Derby. Here she was especially in her element, peering through binoculars with her spectacles perched on her forehead. At one moment she rushed, like an excited schoolgirl, to the rail of the Royal Box to witness a thrilling moment (her horse came in fourth). That few seconds of footage made her seem less remote, and more likeably human, than any Christmas broadcast she has ever delivered.

She was going to need a cheerful nature, for in the same year a bomb exploded under the house of Windsor, metaphorically if not literally. It was the publication of a book, *Diana: Her True Story*, by the journalist Andrew Morton. At first, it had not been taken entirely seriously, and most newspapers had not wished to serialise it, assuming that its contents were speculation or even the inventions of a 'tabloid vulgarian'. The *Sunday Times* eventually agreed to publish parts of Morton's work, and the revelations this offered were to make it one of the two or three most talked-about books of the decade. People read it with horrified fascination.

*Diana: Her True Story* made claims that Diana had been miserable throughout her married life, that her husband had had an affair with his long-term friend Mrs Parker Bowles after their marriage, that she suffered from the eating disorder bulimia and that she had a tendency towards self-harm – indeed, that she had attempted suicide by throwing herself down a flight of stairs at Sandringham. These were extraordinary allegations. The public was astonished to read such things about a woman who seemed to have everything – beauty, health, position, attractive children and a limitless clothing budget. Millions had subscribed to the fairy-tale-come-true image of the Waleses. Could it really be such a sham?

Many people, however, were aware that husband and wife had grown increasingly separate and bitter. Diana was newsworthy where Charles was merely dutiful. She courted the media, he did not ('I'm not very good at being a performing monkey,' he said). She was photographed extravagantly hugging their children; he subscribed to the view that family affection was a private matter. Their differences in outlook and attitude were to become rallying-points once open conflict broke out.

Even if Morton was an experienced royal correspondent, however, and had access to 'inside sources', how could he have discovered so much that was deeply personal? And was he, in any case, a reliable chronicler? It happened that he had, since 1990, been working on a book about Diana. This might have become just another coffee-table ornament had she not authorised others to speak for her. Morton had – readers learned – been given extensive access to her friends, who had described her troubled life in considerable detail. Only after the Princess's death was it revealed that, in fact, it was she herself who had provided most of the information – the posthumous reprint of his book contained dozens of pages of tape transcripts.

By the early 1990s, Diana was in a state of armed rebellion against the Royal Family, the Court and her husband. She

wanted to get her side of the story published, and having a journalist in her proximity provided the opportunity. Although
she wished to do no damage to a throne her son would one
day inherit, she wanted to exact a form of revenge on Charles
and on the Court officials she saw as personal enemies – most
notably her brother-in-law, Robert Fellowes, the Queen's
Private Secretary. She resented the need to live behind a façade
of hypocritical, pretended normality, and wanted the nation to
know what she really had to endure. This was to be the first
volley in what would be dubbed 'the war of the Waleses'.

The Queen was, predictably, horrified. Although it was not
clear to what extent her daughter-in-law had been involved,
it was rank treason to cooperate even indirectly with a book
that presented the entire Family in such a bad light. The lack of
comment from the Palace – this is a standard and effective way
of staying out of disputes – seemed to confirm Morton's allegations. In truth, there was a great deal Her Majesty had not
known about the state of the marriage. The Windsors are capable of great family feeling. Their unique experience and isolation from others can draw them together so that Christmases,
for instance, are boisterous occasions. They do not, however,
share their problems. During years of mounting strife and
estrangement, Charles did not inform the Queen of the full
extent of his difficulties, and she did not ask. She had a strong
aversion to interfering in her children's lives. By the time he
did explain the situation to her, in 1992, it was too late.

It seemed that divorce was the likely outcome, the only solution to a marriage that had become too painful to continue.
The Queen could not countenance this. Not only had she a
strong personal belief in the sanctity of marriage, but it was
also unthinkable that the heir to the throne – the next Supreme
Governor of the Anglican Church – should be separated and
publicly labelled as an adulterer. She contemplated the damage
to the monarchy with even greater disquiet. She doubtless
thought of the millions who had watched the wedding just over

a decade earlier, and who had shown such kindness, loyalty and enthusiasm. These were Charles's future subjects. How could they be let down so badly? How would they react? The monarchy relies on precedent to guide its actions, but there was no precedent for this. And then, of course, there were the personal allegations about Charles that had appeared in the book. He was a highly popular Prince of Wales. Although he lacked the flamboyance of his predecessor, the later Duke of Windsor, he was greatly liked. He was – and is – immensely conscientious. With a passionate concern for social problems and the environment, and the means to exert influence in these areas, he has made a massive contribution to national life. His only perceived fault had been an amiable eccentricity, reflected in a tendency to talk to plants ('How long have you been a tulip?' one cartoonist had him ask). Now for the first time in his life he was beginning to draw hostility as members of the public took sides.

In that year it seemed the entire façade of royal respect-ability wobbled and threatened to come crashing down. In March, Prince Andrew and Sarah Ferguson announced their intention to separate. A matter of weeks later the marriage of Princess Anne and Mark Phillips, who had been apart since 1989, formally ended. Now the relationship of the Waleses was in terminal difficulties and threatened to disintegrate at any moment. The hackneyed term 'dysfunctional' appeared with increasing, predictable frequency in press references to the Family. How could the monarchy survive such a pounding from the media and the public? The Queen met with her eldest son and his wife and urged that they keep trying to reconcile, at least to buy time. Her firmness cowed Diana.

At least with the Yorks there was no apparent animosity. Not only Andrew's naval career but also his newly acquired passion for golf had meant they were too often apart, and Sarah sought diversion. They did, however, remain united by affection for their daughters and a determination to be good parents. Any hope of a reconciliation between them – or the buying of time to spread the burden of bad publicity – was, however, spoiled when in August the *Daily Mirror* printed on its front page a picture of the Duchess having her toes sucked by a man identifiable as her 'financial advisor', an American called John Bryan. Other images made it evident that she was topless and that her girls were nearby. The paper sold out within hours. 'Fergie is Finished!' trumpeted the press. This seemed the single greatest humiliation suffered by any member of the Family within the reach of memory. 'Financial advisor' became a term loaded with smirking innuendo. The Duchess, who was with the Family at Balmoral when the story broke, left there shortly afterwards.

Another tabloid, the *Sun*, published material that had been in its possession for some time. This was the script of a tape-recorded conversation between Diana and James Gilbey, a man with whom she was obviously intimate. He addressed her numerous times by the pet-names 'Squidge', or 'Squidgy', and thus the affair was dubbed 'Squidgygate' by the media . It seemed that the conversation had taken place on New Year's Eve, 1989. Diana was deeply depressed. In the course of reciting her woes she was heard to say: 'I'm going to do something dramatic because I can't stand the confines of this marriage.' Despite this threat, she was not guilty of engineering an embarrassing revelation. It was found, on the contrary, that the most likely source of the leak was a tap on her phone at Sandringham, and it is speculated that this was done by interests favourable to Prince Charles. The discovery that she, too, seemed guilty of adultery cost her at least some of the moral high-ground she had occupied.

And then there were even more revelations. 'Camillagate' was the release in the tabloids of transcripts of a telephone conversation between Charles and Mrs Parker Bowles. Much of the content of this dialogue was highly personal and its publication seemed, for the Prince, an all-but-insurmountable humiliation. What was forgotten, amid the storm of public revulsion, was that no one should have been listening in the first place. 'I know a thing or two about espionage,' said the thriller writer Frederick Forsyth, 'and what is being done to the Royal Family is espionage.'

The most vivid in the series of Royal misfortunes took place that winter. Around mid-morning on 20 November 1992 an electric light bulb, left on too close to a curtain, started a blaze in the private chapel in Windsor Castle, and soon flames were visible on the roof of the Brunswick Tower. The fire lasted 24 hours, doing immense – but thankfully not irreparable – damage to the buildings on the north side of the Castle's Upper Ward. Because these rooms were being rewired, most of the treasures they contained had been removed. Thanks to the quick thinking of staff, almost all the artefacts were saved. Among those who came to the rescue were Prince Andrew, who had been working in the Royal Archives, and the Lord Chamberlain, who personally climbed a ladder to bring down the Lawrence portraits in the Waterloo Chamber. This event proved something of a national trauma. Television news showed a clutter of hosepipes, charred roof-timbers, and soldiers carrying a gigantic, rolled-up carpet. It was much more of a personal tragedy for the Queen, who had driven straight from London on receiving word. She created the lasting image of the day as, dressed in a hooded waterproof coat, she stood among the rubble, peering forlornly at the gutted St George's Hall. This became a photographer's dream – a single image that summed up the situation and became a metaphor for the unhappiness of the monarch. It was understandably much used in reviews of that year. Of her five homes this is the one for which she has the greatest affection. Its destruction set the seal on her misery and would prompt the most famous words she had spoken in public since the address on her 21st birthday.

The destruction could have been so much worse. As, in the photograph, she surveys the damaged hall, it is obvious that the walls are still sound and have not even lost their painted decoration. Had the flames travelled a short distance further and reached the Royal Library, the result would have been a major cultural disaster. As it was, significant casualties amounted to two items: a Victorian sideboard thought to be by Pugin, and a huge painting by Sir William Beechey of George III reviewing troops. (Even this latter was not a complete loss to the nation, since the National Army Museum has a very close copy of the canvas by Beechey's son.) There had been no damage whatever to the parts of the Castle in which the Queen and her family live. Nevertheless, it was tragedy enough. The stench of burnt wood hung over the quadrangle for days, and it was to take five years before the damage was repaired. One of her aides said: 'I don't think I've seen her as emotionally affected by anything as by the Windsor fire.'

But even as clearing up and rebuilding began, her troubles were not over. It was immediately announced by the Secretary of State for National Heritage – before the extent of damage had even been properly estimated – that the repairs to the Castle would be paid for from public funds. The Castle, which of course was not the Queen's personal property but the nation's, had not been insured, and the cost was found to be £37 million. There was outrage that, during a savage recession, the world's richest woman was to be subsidised to this extent. 'When the Castle stands it is theirs,' fumed Janet Daley, one of many critical journalists, 'but when it burns down it is ours.'

The Queen was genuinely, profoundly shocked by the apparent viciousness of these attacks. She had devoted 40 years of her life to selfless public service. She was an exemplary monarch even down to the efforts she made – and which went largely unnoticed – to save taxpayers' money. She did her job well, she knew it, and everyone told her so. Other than a few cranks, she was greeted everywhere she went by smiling faces, and thus could have had no notion that she would be so unpopular. Neither had her Prime Minister,

John Major, who announced the news in the Commons. It was bewildering and extremely hurtful even if, as was usual, she concealed her feelings. Members of her family had made themselves unpopular through their behaviour, but she had not previously had the venom of the public turned on her like this. She has rightly prided herself on her ability to judge the public mood, to understand what her subjects think and want. In the 1990s, however, there were two occasions on which her judgement let her down. The first was her expectation that the public would automatically be willing to pay for the rebuilding of her home. The second was her response to the death of Diana.

Where she *had* read the national mood correctly was in the matter of income tax. Her exemption from this was causing increasing resentment, and she had known for some time that it was necessary to change the way things were done. She was willing, but the matter had not yet been resolved when the fire began. The announcement within days that both she and Prince Charles would pay the tax – though only on public income and not on investments – made it look as if she were frightened of the public.

Only four days after the fire, she made a speech at London's Guildhall that set the seal on her misery. Memorably – and it was indeed her most notable utterance for a generation – she used the phrase *annus horribilis* to describe the previous 12 months, though with characteristic humour she expressed this in understatement: 'This is not a year on which I will look back with undiluted pleasure,' she said. She addressed, indirectly, those who attack the monarchy, from bar-room critics to the newspaper empire of the anti-monarchist Rupert Murdoch, and asked for their indulgence. Like every speech the Queen has ever made, this was written beforehand and read from notes. She does not extemporise, even when speaking from the heart. This was a speech without precedent, a plea for public sympathy.

She said:

'In the words of one of my more sympathetic correspondents it has been an *Annus Horribilis*. History will take a more
moderate view of the events of this year than contemporary
commentators. He who has never failed to reach perfection
has the right to be the sharpest critic. No institution, including
the monarchy, should expect to be free from scrutiny. It can
be just as effective if it is made with a touch of gentleness and
understanding.'

This was unprecedented. Although she had sounded vulnerable before ('I shall not be able to bear the burden . . .'), it was
the first time she had pleaded for her people's compassion, and
it was the nearest she had come to being emotional in any public
statement. As John Major, who was present, was to comment:
'It drew from people an understanding that, monarch or not,
here was someone who wasn't isolated and insulated from the
normal problems and vicissitudes of life.' Although undoubtedly bloodied by the year's events, she remained unbowed. In
public she continued to behave with characteristic stoicism.
Her public duties continued and she smiled as graciously as
ever.

\*      \*      \*

The following autumn, while the Family was at Balmoral,
Buckingham Palace opened to the public for the first time in
its history. Since the dispute over Windsor Castle had ended
with Her Majesty receiving most of the bill, the ticket sales for
one royal residence would now go to pay for the rebuilding
of another. Only the ceremonial areas could be seen, for the
Queen had decided what would be on show, and there would
be no question of any family rooms being open. Tickets were
expensive, and so were the items in the souvenir shop, but

there was no lack of customers either then or thereafter, and the necessary capital began to accumulate.

While this represented a change at home, there were far more significant things happening abroad. The collapse of the Communist Bloc at the end of the 1980s was the biggest change the world had seen since 1945, necessitating a large-scale rethink of commercial, diplomatic and military relations with both allies and former adversaries. As a personification of the older democracies and of Britain's desire to sponsor political and economic development, the Queen was much in evidence. Once Germany had reunited, she visited Berlin and walked through the Brandenburg Gate before laying a wreath at the monument to those killed while trying to cross the Wall. She went to Dresden, a city so heavily damaged by Allied bombing in the war that it was seen as symbol of both the horrors of war and the possibility of reconciliation. Although protesters threw eggs, she presented the community with a replacement weathervane for its *Frauenkirche* – a destroyed and rebuilt church. This had been paid for entirely through funds raised in Britain.

At home she received visitors from the Eastern Bloc – Lech Walesa from Poland and Václav Havel from Czechoslovakia. Not only their countries, but also both of these men in person, had suffered as a result of Soviet control. They must have mused on the good fortune of the British Isles, to whom the narrow defensive ditch of the Channel had given centuries of protection – a place free from outside interference for a thousand years, which greeted official visitors with costumed pomp and whose Head of State had presided over it for longer than any other in Europe. One of these eastern visitors, President Boris Yeltsin of Russia, invited Her Majesty – in the course of lunch at Buckingham Palace – to pay a state visit to Russia.

There are two such visits each year, and they take about two years to arrange. It was 1994 before the Royal Yacht dropped anchor in the Neva, the river on whose islands St Petersburg was built. There are reasons for such a long period of preparation. An itinerary has to be worked out, an exercise that involves the Palace, the host government and the British Embassy. It must be decided in minute detail what Her Majesty will see, the people she will meet and the places she will go. A typical visit would last for three days. It would involve, on arrival, a drive through the capital to let Her Majesty and the populace see each other. There would be visits – extremely brief ones – to museums, factories or other institutions of which her hosts were especially proud. There would be several receptions at which both the eminent and the socially ambitious would meet her for the duration of a brief handshake. There would be a gala theatre performance and there would be a round of calls on hospitals, schools or similarly worthy establishments. In countries with a rich folk tradition, whether in Africa, Asia or Europe, there would be displays of dancing and music. There would also be the returning of hospitality by the Queen, who would give a dinner at her Embassy, at a hotel or – as was commonplace – aboard *Britannia*. For this event, absolutely everything needed – cutlery, crockery, glassware, tablecloths, menus, and so on – will be provided by the Palace. The waiting staff and the chefs will also come from there. The amount of materials involved in such an operation is considerable, and therefore so is the detailed planning that must precede it.

Wherever the Queen is to go, an advance party will investigate. It will work out exactly where she is going and how long it will take to get there – to the minute. She brings her own car and chauffeur, and will be driven slowly so that she can be seen. On her trip to Russia her Rolls-Royce was delivered in advance, but her hosts discovered at the last minute that they had no suitable ramps to unload it. A frantic search of railway sidings, the night before the car was needed, provided what was necessary.

Her staff will visit every place she will stay, measuring doorways and rooms and beds. It will work out the length of time she will stay in each place, how she will enter and exit, and will even factor in the length of speeches. It will take careful note of the colour schemes. She cannot arrive wearing shades that will clash with wallpaper, with the uniforms of a guard of honour or with the sash and ribbon of an order with which she is to be invested – not least because she will be extensively photographed. Meanwhile, at the start of each year while she is at Sandringham, she will begin the extensive reading that is necessary for the visits she will make. She works her way through books, articles, reports – anything her staff feel will help her grasp the essence of the place and the people she is going to meet.

The making and fitting of the clothes she wears will have begun at least a year ahead. As well as avoiding certain colours, her dressmakers will look for ways of paying compliment. This can be done by incorporating the colours of the national flag, or more commonly by having a decorative pattern that incorporates an indigenous flower. Such measures will be taken whether she is going to a foreign country or to one of her own overseas realms. In Canada it can be guaranteed that the maple leaf will appear somewhere, in New Zealand the fern, in Australia the wattle flower. These devices will be particularly noticeable on the evening gowns she wears for state dinners. Otherwise, her wardrobe naturally also has to take account of the climate and the time of year at which she is visiting, as well as making it possible to travel in different types of vehicle – everything from a canoe to a howdah – as well as being easy to do up and to get in and out of, for she will have several changes of clothing a day. Apart from ensuring that she does not wilt in heat or freeze in cold – and also that she is prepared for sudden or unseasonable changes of conditions – garments must as always ensure that she can be seen from a distance.

She also takes with her a number of travel essentials: Malvern water, which she drinks every day; chocolate mints; Dundee cake; Earl Grey tea; her personal kettle; a thermos; a hot water bottle and pillows (how many people cannot sleep comfortably away from home?); barley sugar to ward off travel sickness; and her own soap.

Everything is transported in distinctive blue trunks. Yellow labels are fixed to the Queen's, to mark them out from those of others in her party. There are also hatboxes, jewel-cases and other items. A specialist servant, the Travelling Yeoman, is tasked with looking after the luggage. One of his problems is disembarking the trunks after she has arrived at her destination, and getting them to the Embassy, or the hotel, *before* she reaches it. Fortunately this is not as difficult as it sounds. Welcoming ceremonies and speeches are often lengthy enough to allow a head start.

If she is staying in a hotel, which is not uncommon, an entire floor will be rented for her and her suite. When in 1968 she visited Vienna, 40 rooms of the Imperial Hotel were allocated to her. She and Prince Philip occupied seven of them, their staff – typically there would be about 30 travelling with them – and their baggage had the rest. Her Majesty's rooms were refurnished specially. Not for her the bland decor and reproduction paintings seen even in expensive hotels. Her suite was filled with baroque treasures that had belonged to the Empress Maria Theresa, brought out of government store and magnificent enough to be coveted by any museum. A direct telephone link was installed with Buckingham Palace, and two guards, quite apart from the Queen's own protection officers, were stationed outside all day and night. For her hosts, as for her Household, a visit by the Queen is not something that can be arranged and prepared for in the space of a few days.

She has, of course, minimal opportunity to enjoy her surroundings or the facilities. Whatever the furnishings in a hotel suite, she will spend very little time there. Every morning she will be out early and will return late. She will have official engagements all day, because on a three- or five-day visit there is so much to be done. She will have speeches to make that may require last-minute revision, and she will have to change clothes several times.

She is extremely adept at this. She can put on a hat without needing a mirror, and can finish dressing while running downstairs. Her clothing is designed with a minimum of awkward catches and buttons so that she can replace one outfit with another swiftly and with the least time and effort. She has with her on every overseas visit two dressers and a hairdresser. Her make-up is applied only sparingly, due to a naturally pure skin, but her lipstick must not be smudged – no matter the circumstances. Her hair must likewise stay in place regardless of how many hats she has taken off and put on, and no matter what the temperature. Because she has only minutes, or even seconds, in which to change clothes or otherwise prepare between events, there is no margin for error. Delays and mistakes are a luxury that cannot be afforded. Time spent looking for the gloves she needs would delay her appearance and the knock-on effect of this could spoil the whole day. Such a mishap could also annoy her, and that too might adversely affect the occasion. Everything must be perfect, not because the Queen is a highly demanding employer but because her own timetable is so utterly unforgiving. If the hat or the umbrella she needs is not being held out ready for her by someone, her appearance may be spoiled and those who have attended it will feel disappointed.

While the Queen's staff plan for every contingency, there are sometimes mishaps. Notorious in the annals of royal travel was her state visit to Morocco in 1989, when the king kept her waiting for over three hours in the heat on her arrival.

Two of her visits during the 1990s were of special significance. In Russia she stayed in the Kremlin, a fortress in the centre of Moscow whose very name evokes chilling memories of the Cold War. Before the Revolution it was a place of pilgrimage and Her Majesty participated in a service, with the Orthodox Metropolitan of Moscow, in one of its several cathedrals. She had several reasons for finding this a moving experience. The Romanovs, the murdered family of the Tsar, were relations of hers, and she had heard stories of them from her grandmother and from Lord Mountbatten. She had also lived through the decades of East–West confrontation as a Head of State. Knowing better than most the dangers to peace during that time, she could marvel at the fact that war had not come. Devoutly religious, she could appreciate that the Christian Church in Russia had survived and flourished despite decades of disapproval and active persecution. Small wonder that she spoke of this event in her Christmas broadcast that year.

*    *    *

There was another bright moment the following year she visited South Africa, for the first time since 1947. After long years of defiant isolation, the country had abandoned its Apartheid government, become a fully democratic country and been readmitted to the Commonwealth. South Africa had played a minor but significant part in her life and she was delighted to see it again, knowing that an issue which had poisoned Commonwealth relations during the 1980s was laid to rest. Nelson Mandela was now President, and had gained immense international respect for his lack of bitterness towards a regime that had imprisoned him for 27 years. A man of legendary warmth, charm and humour, he would be impossible not to like, and his friendship was much-courted by fashionable liberals. He and the Queen had a genuine and unmistakeable mutual admiration, and she must have found him refreshingly unlike any world statesman with whom she had previously dealt. She brought with her, and gave him, the Order of Merit, an award that is entirely in her personal gift and independent of government recommendation. The only other non-British recipients in recent times have been those two other secular saints of the 20th century – Albert Schweitzer and Mother Theresa.

However popular the Queen had been abroad, the monarchy was in the doldrums at home, with the behaviour of the younger Royals still commanding the headlines. In the middle of the decade came the 50th anniversary of the end of the Second World War. This was to be a national celebration, at which the Family – and especially the Queen and Queen Mother – were to be highly visible. It was speculated by those planning the event, that, with the unpopularity of the monarchy, the turnout would be low. Some suggested that to avoid embarrassment it should be held on a modest scale. But just as with every time this argument had been used since 1947, the pessimists were proved wrong. Hyde Park had been envisaged as the venue, but was felt perhaps to be too big and thus liable to look embarrassingly empty. On the day itself – 8 May – it was packed. This celebration, in any case, focused on the older generation of the Family, and not on their errant offspring. It reminded the public of the service given the country by the Queen and her mother. Recent troubles had, in any case, brought the Queen a great deal of sympathy from across the country and the world. The Queen Mother, with her two daughters, appeared on the Palace balcony just as they had a half-century earlier and, in the course of the celebrations, they sang with the rest of the audience the wartime songs. When one of those who led the singing, Cliff Richard, complimented the Queen Mother on remembering the words, she answered: 'We've been rehearsing this for about three weeks.'

In November 1995 the last nail was put in the coffin of the Wales's marriage. The previous year, Charles had participated in a televised interview with the broadcaster Jonathan Dimbleby, who had written a magisterial biography of the Prince. The picture it gave of Charles's parents – his father a no-nonsense bully and his mother preoccupied with affairs of state – was not a flattering one. He himself was presented as an extremely well-meaning man who was doing his best for the country and the monarchy, who was sensitive to social issues and who had an ingrained sense of decency and fairness. The programme was largely remembered, however, for the simple fact that he admitted adultery on television. Now Diana hit back with the same weapon. She too gave an interview, to the BBC current-affairs programme *Panorama*. Everything about it suggested calculation, including her use of black eye-liner to increase the soulful look with which she regarded the audience. Her delivery was halting, emotional, heartbroken. No one could argue that she was not a wronged woman, but she too admitted adultery, with a Household Cavalry officer. She went on to say that she did not think her husband was fit to become King. Whatever sympathy the Princess garnered from this, to have the future queen insulting her husband in public was undoubtedly an ugly and upsetting episode. She said afterwards that she regretted it and she was deeply contrite about any pain caused to the Queen, whom she genuinely respected, but she had gone into this fully aware of what she was doing. For her mother-in-law, Diana's appearance to plead her cause in every sitting room in the country was a measure that could simply not be ignored. It had even happened on the Queen's wedding anniversary. The day after the programme was broadcast, Diana and Charles were written to by Her Majesty and asked to divorce. There was no point trying to keep up appearances when the public now knew all about their animosity. Damage limitation must begin at once before this situation could further threaten the monarchy.

Their separation became final eight months later. Diana, no longer HRH but still a princess, became a celebrity in her own right and a campaigner for good causes. She was quickly removed from the world of the Royal Family – all souvenirs bearing her image at once vanished from the gift shops of royal palaces on the orders of the Queen – although her hold on public affection remained, and she was in no doubt about her ability to win support. She was especially popular in America, whose people have never been able to relate to the Royal Family's unemotional public style or to appreciate how useful this is. The public there sided with her to such an extent that the USA became 'Diana territory'. She went there several times. Charles did not go at all.

At home, opinion was divided into two camps. Traditionalists sided with Charles – he, after all, was the one who was Royal – because they respected his essential integrity and his unde-monstrative manner. They viewed Diana as hysterical and self-centred. To others, she was a saint and martyr. Those of modern outlook saw her as a victim of Establishment bullies who had tried to silence her ('She won't go quietly,' she herself had warned). Every divorced, wronged woman in the coun-try empathised with her. So did the froth of the showbusi-ness world, and the people who sang the songs to which she had danced or made the clothes she wore. This was a cultural conflict between an older, stiff-upper-lip Britain and a new one obsessed with appearance and celebrity. The country braced for a continuing, bruising war of attrition.

The Yorks separated, but this was as amicable as the Wales's split had been acrimonious. Dubbed 'the world's happiest divorced couple', they remained close friends. The Duchess had continued to be an embarrassment. Prince Philip had described her as 'pointless' while the Queen's Private Secretary, Martin Charteris, had famously summed her up with the words 'Vulgar! Vulgar! Vulgar!' Her extravagance – and consequent debts – were a cause for concern, as was her blunt, outspoken manner and willingness to talk to the media about her life within the Family. To the older generation it was inexplicable and horrifying that, instead of keeping their problems to themselves, the younger ones should parade them in the national media. Such openness did them little good.

Respect for the monarchy was crumbling, and increasingly often – in pubs and newspapers – was heard the view that the Crown should 'skip a generation' so that William would be the next king.

\*       \*       \*

Suddenly, unpredictably, the war between Charles and Diana was over. It ended on an August night while the Family was at Balmoral. It was as great a shock to them as it was to the rest of the world, but this did not show and was not perceived. Balmoral is a holiday home and, while they are there, the Family are not often seen outside the walls of the estate. Had they been in London, they would perhaps have made some public gesture. As it was, they remained out of sight. This did not mean they were not grieving, merely that they could not be seen to be doing so.

Public opinion was as fickle as always. Throughout that summer there had been much adverse press comment on the Princess's lifestyle as she was photographed romping in the Mediterranean, and her flirtation with a man many considered unsuitable had lost her much credibility. A cartoon in the *Daily Telegraph*, in which an exhausted housewife sighs 'I really need a break – from reading about Diana's holidays', summed up an attitude that was widespread. When discussing her future as an ex-Royal, one commentator had suggested than within a decade she would be 'just another has-been celebrity living in California', while another predicted her second marriage to 'a Colorado ski-instructor'. When she died, such criticism melted instantly away. Suddenly it seemed deeply churlish to have begrudged her the right to happiness. Such was the outpouring of grief that any negative attitude was seen as insensitive and spiteful. Her death was so sudden that people were in shock for days afterwards. Tributes piled up in such numbers that florists could not keep up with demand.

They carpeted the ground outside the palaces where she had lived and – absurdly – were put on war memorials throughout the country. In death, Diana had won the 'War of the Waleses' – at least until public opinion settled down again – and the Royal Family were cast as villains. In this atmosphere of hysteria the truth did not matter, only people's perceptions. The Princess's parents-in-law had cast her out. They had then compounded their cruelty by failing to mourn. The day after her death – a Sunday – was one of the few times they could be seen at Balmoral, since they attended church at nearby Crathie. It was therefore noticed that they gave no sign of grief, made no comment and even that – astonishingly – the sermon made no reference to the event.

The Queen's attitude was that the death was first and foremost a family tragedy and that it should be dealt with in private. Her greatest concern was for her grandsons, who must be protected, and that normality must be preserved as much as possible. To an extent that many people considered inappropriate, this involved business as usual – carrying on with the sporting pursuits of the season apparently as if nothing had happened. It was days before a mounting tide of press outrage, demanding that Her Majesty 'come back and lead the nation's mourning' ('Show us You Care', said one headline), convinced her to return. She had never experienced a situation like this, and she had been completely wrong-footed. She was roundly blamed for failing to have a national flag flown at half-mast from the palace, even though *no* flag other than the Royal Standard was ever seen there. One could not argue points of protocol with a public that was out for blood, and she authorised the change that opinion demanded. It was also said that she had vetoed the idea of a state funeral because Diana was no longer a member of the Family. The truth was that, since no funeral had taken place in these circumstances before, those planning it had no idea what to do. Again the monarchy's usual standby – precedent: the long-established, long-practised rules for public ceremonies – was of no help. The procedure had to be made up more or less on the spot, and rehearsed with frightening speed.

Having permitted the Union Flag to be hoisted in commemoration of Diana's death, the Queen has allowed it to be flown over the Palace ever since when she is not in residence – a direct and conspicuous sign of having bowed to public opinion. One can sympathise with her sense of hurt in this matter. The British people have always enjoyed the meticulous way in which their monarchy observes the details of pomp and ritual. Its strict adherence to arcane rules makes public spectacle more splendid and creates a mystique that no other Royal House can boast. Her subjects have been proud of this, yet now it became the very thing that caused them anger. No wonder she found the reaction bewildering.

Yet her presence at once began to turn the tide. Returning to London the day before the funeral, the sight of her car coming down Constitution Hill caused spontaneous applause from the large crowd in front of the Palace. The 'walkabout' immediately undertaken by the Queen and her husband to examine the flowers and read inscriptions began to repair the damage. She made a broadcast inside the building, through whose windows the crowd could be seen. It is said that the future of the monarchy hung in the balance during that week, but this is a huge exaggeration. Had the Queen been genuinely unpopular, public opinion would not have forgiven her so swiftly. Once she was seen to be back doing her duty (though she would return to Balmoral the following week), once she had addressed the people 'as your queen and as a grandmother', admitting that: 'there are lessons to be drawn from her life and from the extraordinary reaction to her death', and once she could be seen mourning – the next day she bowed as Diana's coffin passed her – her position was quickly restored. The Princess's death was a tragedy and will always be seen as such, but the Queen's quiet dignity was not as inappropriate as some believed. Once again, she represented timeless values against the fashion of the moment.

Her Majesty was to change little about her public personality, and that was a good thing. The hysteria subsided after a time and left some of the greatest zealots feeling rather foolish. Plans for a statue never came to fruition. The suggestion that Heathrow Airport be renamed in her honour was quietly ignored, as was the notion that August bank holiday be re-named 'Diana Day'. The monarch was seen to have learned the necessary lessons, and after all her style of behaviour, always admired, had perhaps been more appropriate than she was given credit for. The Royal Household had established a committee called the Way Ahead Group to review their strategy of visits and functions so as to make them more responsive to public expectations. It was assumed that this body suggested ways of seeming more informal and approachable, and it has certainly been noticeable that one sees far more pictures of the Queen enjoying herself than used to be the case. Palace receptions can be less formal than they were – with the Queen and her family mingling, just as they do at garden parties. The Palace set up its own website and the Queen has subsequently appeared on Facebook. She has since been seen visiting a McDonald's as well as a pub, being shown round the set of *Eastenders* and attending rehearsals for a West End production of *Oklahoma*.

Those who think this evidence that Her Majesty has 'turned over a new leaf' are mistaken. These are things she has always done. Although she may not be familiar with fast-food outlets she has certainly been in pubs before, though admittedly of the rural, beams-and-fireplace sort found in the Home Counties. As for *Oklahoma*, she knew the show very well since she had been taken to see it by Philip during her courting days, and had at that time had pleasure in playing on the piano one of the songs: 'People Will Say We're in Love'. What has changed is that her travels and her work have been given more positive emphasis. We are reminded, for it is easy in the course of a long reign to forget, how much she does and how much she appears to enjoy it. We are also reminded that, though she may often look solemn and cheerless, her personal restraint is part of a discipline that has enabled her to rule extremely well, and has given her the toughness to master crises that might well have overcome a lesser personality. If these qualities make her seem 'out of date' or 'out of touch', so what? They have been what she and the country needed.

Since August 1997 she has also sought to remind her people that they are not a nuisance, and serving them is a privilege as well as an obligation. In the speech she made at her 50th wedding anniversary she was at pains to stress this: 'It is you who have seen us through and helped to make our duty fun. We are deeply grateful to you . . .'

One thing that helped heal the wounds of the recent past was that Diana's death ended the bickering. Had she lived, the snubs and the sniping and the taking of sides would have gone on for decades. No matter where she had lived or whom she had next married, her royal past would have followed her. The continuing bitterness was a source of anguish and embarrassment for the British people and, whatever the rights and wrongs of the situation, it was doing great damage to the monarchy and the country.

＊    ＊    ＊

A grief of a different kind visited the Family with the decommissioning of *Britannia* – on grounds of expense, because the cost of modernisation was too great – in 1997, after it had travelled more than a million miles. There was some criticism that the Family seemed to mourn the Yacht more than the late Princess. One author noticed that: 'As Her Majesty left the Royal Yacht for the last time, there were tears in her eyes, never seen before. The Queen had allowed her emotions for the old ship to betray her.' *Britannia* had become closer to the hearts of the Royal family than any piece of machinery could be expected to do. Linked with her father, because he had approved its design before his death, and launched more or less as she became Queen, they had begun their official careers together. It was associated with numerous holidays and royal honeymoons as well as with official visits. In port it served as a floating embassy, the venue for numerous banquets and receptions. More importantly, it was a sort of seagoing Balmoral – a home in which the Queen could entirely relax because it offered such privacy. With miles of ocean all around her it was safe from the lenses of press photographers. Anyone could be expected to show sadness at leaving such a familiar friend.

*     *     *

A few months before the end of the 1990s – on 19 June 1999 – the Queen's youngest son was married. This was an event in stark contrast to the extravagant occasions of the previous decade. Now that every one of his siblings was divorced, it seemed perhaps inappropriate to draw too much attention to Prince Edward's wedding. It took place at St George's Chapel in Windsor Castle. The groom, now created Earl of Wessex, arrived on foot with his two brothers from their home in the Upper Ward a few yards away. He wore no uniform, merely a tailcoat. The bride, Sophie Rhys-Jones, a 34-year-old who worked in public relations, likewise had no train, and arrived in a simple but sleek white suit-dress. The guests were brought in by minibus. Apart from the grandness of the building itself, this could have been the wedding of any young middle-class couple of prosperous parentage. One of the guests, the actor Anthony Andrews (who reported that the Queen did the twist at the celebrations afterwards), commented that: 'You felt that you were part of a family occasion, rather than a state one.' A reminder that, whatever their problems, the Royal Family are just like us. They get over their difficulties and carry on.

# MATRIARCH, 2000–2012

'I do like happy endings.'

Although the century should not have begun until 1 January 2000, the Government had decided to start the 'third millennium' 12 months early, with celebrations beginning on New Year's Eve, 1999. The Millennium Dome in Greenwich, a colossal indoor space that was to be filled with quasi-educational sideshows, would be the setting for the launch of the new era. Its construction rushed through and its paintwork barely dry when the day arrived, the building was to symbolise the new beginning in national life that Tony Blair's Labour Government had promised. It proved an apt metaphor for the country's rulers – disdainful of tradition, dismissive of the past, obsessed with novelty, gimmickry and – in the name of 'inclusiveness' – intent on reducing culture to the lowest common denominator. Like so much that was to follow, it would prove tawdry and vapid, and would disappoint millions. On the night, the arena was crowded – though a number of those invited could not get there owing to complications with the rail service. The Queen and Prince Philip, who would not normally have been in London, had agreed to attend. They sat next to the Blairs and, at midnight, were obliged to stand up, join hands and take part in singing 'Auld Lang Syne'. They are not given to demonstrative public behaviour, and pictures of them at that moment reveal a stiff awkwardness. Blair himself recorded in his memoirs that: 'I don't know what Prince Philip thought of it all, but I shouldn't imagine it's printable. I suspect Her Majesty would have used different language but with the same sentiment.' Shortly afterwards they escaped to Sandringham.

Perhaps they felt they owed something to Blair. In the days that followed Diana's death it was conjectured that the public mood would have been hostile enough to have banished the monarchy, had the Prime Minister not been supportive of it. This is nonsense. You cannot undo an entire constitutional system overnight, and no sizeable or influential body of opinion had wanted to. Nevertheless his refusal to endorse the anti-royalist views of some in his government had gone some way to defusing the hysteria of the moment.

A more successful celebration, in August 2000, was that of the Queen Mother's 100th birthday. The biggest event, in a series of commemorations, was held on Horse Guards Parade. Organised by Major Michael Parker, a military impresario responsible for innumerable tattoos, it involved the charities of which she was patron, the regiments with which she was connected and a wealth of other groups, organisations, representatives – and animals. There were chickens and cattle in the procession that passed in front of Her Majesty, for every aspect of her life was to be reflected. On the day itself – 4 August – there was some amusement when she received from her daughter the customary message of congratulations sent to every centenarian: 'The Queen is much interested to hear that you are celebrating your one hundredth birthday, and sends you warm congratulations and good wishes.'

\*    \*    \*

For the Royal Family, as for the rest of the world, the new century effectively began on 11 September 2001. They were at Balmoral, and will have followed the events on television, as did countless others. Among the dead there were many subjects of the Queen, and she will have shared in full the general sense of shock and grief. The events of that day heralded the advent of a new age of international terror just as the old era of more local terrorism was ending. With the Good Friday Agreement, peace had largely returned to Ulster and it was hoped that the Omagh bomb – which ripped through a pretty market town in the summer of 1998, becoming one of the worst atrocities in Ulster's history – was the bloody climax to a campaign of violence that had achieved nothing. Now those who protected the Queen, and the public, had to look for danger from a new direction. The British were long used to anti-terrorist precautions. By now they were scarcely shocked, or surprised, by the number of policemen carrying sidearms, or even machine guns, in the streets.

Amid the climate of fearful disbelief that followed the attacks of 11 September, there were some symbolic gestures the monarch could make. She authorised, on the day of mourning, the playing of 'The Star-spangled Banner' during the changing of the guard at Buckingham Palace. In attendance were Prince Andrew and the US Ambassador, while outside the railings were numbers of expatriate Americans, perhaps enabled to feel linked with home. The Queen visited New York, went to Ground Zero, attended a commemorative service, and awarded the city's dynamic mayor, Rudolph Giuliani, the KBE for his leadership during the crisis. As so often, she could seem a personification of stability, continuity and normality, even outside her own realms.

These realms were gearing up to mark her Golden Jubilee in the summer of 2002. This time more than ever, in view of the drubbing the Royal Family's reputation had endured in the previous decade, official opinion was hesitant about the scale of celebrations. Would a large event be too ambitious? Would the Mall look embarrassingly empty if not enough people turned out? It seems to be customary to 'fly a kite' in these circumstances: the Palace makes it known, several months ahead, that the celebrations for a Royal event will be modest. It then waits for public reaction. As disappointment and complaint grow louder, the preparations expand accordingly. In this case, it was obvious during the spring that momentum was building, and it was decided that there would be a four-day commemoration, spread over a weekend at the end of May and beginning of June. There would be a procession to St Paul's, a thanksgiving service, a balcony appearance, fireworks – all the things that people hope for and expect.

Just as the festivities were being planned, the Family was struck by tragedy. Princess Margaret had been an increasingly shadowy presence in public life since the traumas of the 1970s. She had been the first of the Royals to lose dignity as a result of scandal, and her standing had never really recovered. Her health had also been failing. She had suffered bronchitis and laryngitis. A smoker, like her father, she had – like him – undergone a lung operation. In 1998 she had a stroke. She subsequently, and badly, scalded her feet in a bath. She had a second stroke. By the time she was seen on the occasion of the Queen Mother's 100th birthday she was a pitiable figure, confined to a wheelchair, expressionless and apparently speechless, her eyes hidden by sunglasses. She was in great pain, and confided to a friend that she longed 'to join Papa'. On 9 February – three days after the anniversary of his own death – she did. Following a third stroke she was taken to hospital, where she died. Confirming her reputation as the most unconventional member of the Family, she had asked to be cremated at the Slough municipal crematorium, the nearest such facility to Windsor. It was a gesture of defiant individualism, a final act of rebellion against a position in life that had so signally failed to bring her happiness.

The Queen Mother, too, was visibly declining. She refused to be defeated by age or infirmity, insisting on entertaining guests or making visits despite having to walk, slowly and painfully, with sticks. She seemed to keep going entirely by willpower, but then this had always been her defining quality. It had enabled her to lead the monarchy's fight-back after the Abdication, to transform her shy husband into a hugely popular King, and to be a mother to the nation during the Second World War. Hitler had called her 'the most dangerous woman in Europe'. Among less biased observers – and her former subjects – her popularity was limitless, as was the love they had for her. In 2001 her great-grandson William had called on her before going off to university. 'Any good parties, be sure and let me know!' she had allegedly told him. This was among her last recorded statements. It was cherished by the public as evidence of a sparkling sense of fun that combined with an unquenchable, uncrushable spirit. But this could not compensate for physical frailty. Her last days were spent at Royal Lodge, the home in Windsor that she and her husband had first occupied in the 1920s. Aware that time was running out, she punctiliously spent her days in thanking those who had been her friends, or had looked after her, over the years. It was a charming, touching way for anyone to leave the world. Her last moments came on Easter Saturday, in the afternoon. The Queen, who had been riding in the Park, went at once to her bedside and was there when she died.

These events marked the end of an age in a way that nothing had done since the King himself had died 50 years earlier. The Queen was now the only survivor of the tightly bound unit her father had dubbed 'we four'. Although he had died at 56, the Queen has otherwise been extremely fortunate in that those closest to her have lived long. Her sister was 71, her mother was 101. Her husband has reached 90 without seriously slowing down. To those who are so blessed, losses perhaps seem keener. Her Majesty received immense public sympathy, and there was widespread grief. A million people stood in the streets to see the Queen Mother's coffin pass, or waited for up to nine hours to view her coffin in Westminster Hall. Throughout the troubled 1990s, monarchists had been well aware that the death of the Queen Mother would focus public affection once more on the virtues of royalty – would provide the most effective counter-blow against the tide of criticism and trivialisation – and there had been a certain guilty impatience for this moment to come. It had fulfilled their expectations. 'These are times,' wrote the *Guardian*'s Jonathan Friedland, 'when republicans should walk humbly.'

Despite this national mourning, the Jubilee went ahead as envisaged. Her Majesty made tours of Commonwealth countries, and visited the four parts of the United Kingdom. On 4 June 2002, she travelled with her husband to St Paul's in the Coronation Coach. Over a million waited along the route, on a damp and overcast morning, to see her. As always, the British cherish these occasions. They love to revel in the feeling that their ceremonial is more ancient, more elaborate, better planned and prepared and better performed than any other public occasions, anywhere. They are not only there to glimpse, or acclaim, the sovereign; they are also congratulating themselves on how well their country celebrates. The Queen set off from the Palace dressed in sky blue. When she returned, hours later, the weather had changed and so had she, for she was now in pink. As she stood on the Palace balcony she could see that, beyond the Victoria Memorial, the Mall was a solid mass of people all the way to the distant Admiralty Arch. A sea of miniature Union Flags flapped and waved like a multi-coloured blizzard; larger banners, of Scotland, England and Wales, were draped on shoulders or lamp posts, or flourished exuberantly. 'Land of Hope and Glory', sung over and over again, was loud enough for the words to be audible inside the Palace. The Queen responded to cheering with repeated, gentle waves of her black-gloved hand and a smile that indicated quiet, modest but genuine pleasure. The possibility of looking down at the populace and feeling the force of mass affection is something only a highly popular Head of State can know. Even though she does this once a year on her official birthday, the scene that day must surely have been one of the great experiences of her life.

In the sky, far to the east, there were distant specks that grew bigger as the seconds passed. Aircraft in tight formation aligned on the Mall. Now the sound of them caused the crowd to look up. The Red Arrows, the RAF's aerobatic team, shot over their heads with a reverberating roar, leaving a hanging trail of red, white and blue smoke. Ahead of them, the scream of its engines so loud that it drowned even the noise from the thousands below, was the sleek white shape of Concorde. Its sharp nose lifted gracefully as it peeled off and climbed towards the stratosphere. Hundreds of thousands gasped, and then cheered.

The Golden Jubilee was a very different experience from the ceremonial events of 1977. The procession that had followed Her Majesty back to the Palace – she and Prince Philip had returned standing up in an open Land Rover – included more than the bands and marching dignitaries that onlookers expected, and the atmosphere was noticeably more informal and light-hearted, more like that of a student rag-procession than a state occasion. The public took away memories of elaborate West Indian carnival costumes, pumping rock music, VC winners travelling in a vintage car, and a giant pony-tailed 'caring dad' with infant strapped to his chest. Another change since the 1970s was that members of the Royal Family (though not the monarch herself) had come out of the Palace the evening before the celebrations to meet some of those who were sitting all night on the kerbsides. Since the 100th-birthday celebrations for the Queen Mother, it seems there has been a hint of quirky eccentricity in the planning of popular Royal occasions. The notion of a rock musician, Brian May, playing 'God Save the Queen' on electric guitar on the roof of the Palace that evening (there was a concert for the public in the gardens) was a gesture that captured the imagination of millions around the world, and showed that for all its perceived irrelevance to the 'modern world', Royalty can harness elements of mass-culture for its own purposes.

However impressed Her Majesty was by Concorde's tribute – and she apparently loved it – she will have felt nothing but relief when, the year after her Jubilee, its flights ended. By accident of circumstance the United Kingdom's biggest and busiest airport is within a few miles of Windsor Castle. An extremely old joke has it that a tourist asks why the Castle was built so close to the airport. While the location may be convenient for travel both for the Queen and for her visitors, there is no doubt that it is more a blight than a blessing. Since the development of the jet engine in the 1950s the Castle's occupants have had to accustom to an increasing level of noise-pollution from aircraft departing and landing, and in this they share the experience of millions of citizens who live to the west of London. On the two occasions each day that Concorde came in to land, seeming to hover over the town of Windsor like some malevolent bird of prey, the noise of its engines was deafening – virtually loud enough to drown out a brass band.

There have been other celebrations since the Golden Jubilee, and it appears that Royal hospitality, always impressive, is gaining an element of imagination too. Already the Queen and Prince Philip had had the notion of celebrating their 50th wedding anniversary with a garden party for other couples who had 'tied the knot' in the year 1947. Even more charming was the Queen's 80th birthday celebration. This, too, was held in the gardens of Buckingham Palace, but the guests were 2,000 children – as well as a host of characters from children's literature and television. A specially written play was put on with a cast of celebrities, entitled *The Queen's Handbag*. In the story, this most famous of Royal accessories is stolen, but is restored to her at the end. 'Oh good,' said Her Majesty, who was also watching the performance. 'I do like happy endings.'

In her eighties, the Queen remains fixed in habit. She spends the year in the same places, doing the same things (though sadly she has had to give up riding). She likes Earl Grey tea, and German wines but not champagne (both she and Prince Philip only pretend to sip it during toasts). She does not eat pasta because the sauces are likely to be messy, and avoids shellfish because of the possible ill-effects. She likes simple food because she has to eat so much elaborate fare on official occasions. Being of a frugal nature, she expects the leftovers from Palace meals to be utilised for days afterwards. She allegedly does not like facial hair – or waistcoats – on men. She drives herself when she is on private roads within her estates, but does not wear a safety belt (which is not illegal on such thoroughfares) and regularly exceeds the speed limit. On at least two occasions members of the public have been put to flight by Her Majesty bearing down on them, at an estimated 60, and 70, miles an hour where she should have been doing 30. In one of these instances she had her Private Secretary send a note of apology. Her speeding, like her refusal to wear a hard hat when riding, is an oddly rebellious aspect of a personality that is otherwise both cautious and conventional.

Although members of the Royal Family often feel that press attention is a nuisance, they are well aware that they nevertheless need it. If journalists did not write about them and the public did not read about them, monarchy might die by neglect. The Queen, understandably, likes to know what is being said about her and can be irritated if coverage seems inadequate, just as she likes the applause of the public. After the annual Trooping the Colour ceremony she appears with her family on the Palace balcony, and is greeted by large crowds because the police, controlling the movement of people below, let them into the area in time to reach the Palace railings as she appears. A few years ago she was annoyed with the senior police officer in charge because the crowd was held back for too long and she came onto the balcony to find no one there.

She is greatly attached to Windsor, Balmoral and Sandringham. This latter, a Victorian building described – with some justification – as looking like a 'Scottish golf hotel', is the place in which she can come closest to the life of a farmer's wife that she coveted as a girl. Her estate grows commercial crops – such as blackcurrants that end up in Ribena – and she is president of the local Women's Institute, as her mother was before her. Her neighbours and tenants include people whose families she has known through generations. It has often been asked, since her accession, why she does not spend more time in her overseas realms. It was seriously suggested, in the 1960s, that she live for some weeks every year in Canada. The problem is that if she did so, Australia and New Zealand would then ask why she could not do the same there, and the structure of her life would quickly unravel. In London she is in close contact with all her overseas dominions through their High Commissions, and can respond at once to events. The only concession she has been willing to make is to spend part of the month of June at Holyrood in Edinburgh, and this is in any case the country where she goes on holiday.

When at Buckingham Palace – and that is where most of her time is spent – she awakens at 7:30, when her tea is brought. Her dogs are, meanwhile, being walked in the gardens. She breakfasts an hour later, alone with Prince Philip, and reads the *Daily Telegraph*. While she does so, a piper plays outside for 15 minutes. This was a tradition started by Victoria, and it is not popular with every member of the Household. As one author put it, 'it is a sound that inspires no apathy'.

Her dogs – she has something in the region of 30 corgis – have their own accommodation next to the Page's pantry. She likes to put their food out herself. She is naturally fond of them, but few members of her staff share this enthusiasm.

Corgis can be vicious – biting, fighting and making messes on the carpets – and many pages and footmen over the years have borne the scars of their ill-temper. Although undoubtedly a dog-lover, she does not care for cats. When someone once gave her a Siamese, it was very quickly passed on to a new home.

Her mornings are given over to administration. Her Private Secretary brings documents that need her signature, as well as a summary of the day's news and cuttings relating to the Royal Family. She also examines her mail. Her Majesty receives letters at the rate of 2,000–3,000 a day. She glances at the envelopes and chooses 12 or so that she will open. After long years of practice, she has an instinct for finding those that will prove interesting. The ones that need a written reply are passed on to a lady-in-waiting or to her Private Secretary. Some missives are from cranks, many are simply good wishes, a surprising number are asking for help with problems, and, where appropriate, these are sent to the relevant government departments. If the Queen is writing to friends – and she is a regular and disciplined correspondent – she uses green ink to signify that it is a personal letter.

Her audiences take place at around noon, typically last a matter of 10 minutes or so, and involve making small-talk with a variety of visitors – ambassadors, clerics, academics and senior officers. There is not time to deal with any subject in detail, and the Queen's reticence has led some of those she received to confess that keeping the conversational ball in the air was a struggle. Once again, however, it is not what she said but the fact that she met with them that is important.

She normally lunches by herself, or with Prince Philip if he is not busy with his own duties, in the bow-windowed sitting room that faces towards Green Park. She chooses her meals at the beginning of every week from a list of suggestions prepared by the chef, so she always knows what to expect. After lunch she walks with her dogs in the gardens. She likes to be alone, so staff must stay out of her sight. There follows a brief interlude with the racing papers, and then further business, perhaps involving a visit somewhere. Whatever she is doing, she will have finished before five o'clock so that she can have tea, which is her favourite meal. The miniature sandwiches and Dundee cake are the same every day, as are the scones – which she feeds to her dogs. If it is Tuesday she will have her weekly visit from the Prime Minister at 6:30, and this will last until about seven o'clock. If she has no evening engagement, she may dine with her husband and then spend an hour or more with her boxes. She reads every evening a summary of the day's events in Parliament. After that, she will perhaps watch television or work on a jigsaw. She retires at about 11.

It remains a paradox that, for all her shyness when making small talk (Blair described her as being both reticent and direct), she is competent, professional and a pleasure to meet. Helen Mirren, fêted for her screen portrayal of Her Majesty, expressed to a Hollywood public her conversion from sceptic to admirer. Those who are themselves accomplished professionals – and perhaps especially if they are in performing or public-relations professions – recognise the quality of what the Queen does, her dedication and stamina and focus.

She is an extremely accomplished and thoughtful hostess. When she dines with others she is always served first, yet when she finishes everyone else has their plates cleared away. Experienced courtiers therefore waste no time in talking to their neighbours – there will be time for that afterwards – and concentrate on eating. The Queen is aware of the problem, however, and may well have a salad beside her which she will make a pretence of eating in order to allow the other guests more time.

Those who go to Windsor to 'dine and sleep' – short visits by groups of 10 prominent people that involve staying the night – will find that attention to detail characteristic of Royal occasions is evident here, too, and that the Queen is personally responsible for much of it. She will have inspected the rooms in which they are to stay, checking that everything they need has been provided, and she will choose books for their bedside tables. Given an audience of people with whom she has some chance to interact she is far more humorous, vivacious and animated than when merely shaking hands. Given a subject on which to discourse – the Castle and its contents – she is lively, anecdotal and entertaining. Apart from a lifetime's association with it, she has seriously studied its contents. It is usual practice, after dinner, to take guests round the Royal Library to show them something of the collections. This is, in fact, much more of a full-blown museum than its name suggests, for it contains many three-dimensional objects, such as a collection of walking sticks, an array of British and foreign orders, the flying gloves worn by Prince Andrew in the Falklands campaign – and a bread roll dating from Victoria's Diamond Jubilee. Items will have been chosen for display because they reflect the interests of particular guests, and there is bound to be something that will capture the imagination, or at least seize the attention, of everyone present. This may well involve more than merely getting a few volumes off a shelf. If a guest has an interest in antique swords or armour, it may take a team of several men to clean, prepare and arrange the necessary heavy and awkward exhibits.

When her guests at Windsor are fellow Heads of State, management of the event will naturally be just as flawless. Her Majesty will have taken a great deal of interest in the preparation of St George's Hall for the state dinner, discussing the menu and the flower arrangements and the seating plan long in advance. Once again, the way in which things are done by the Queen and her Household sets a standard for other countries. Ronald Reagan said that: 'The state visit to Britain is one of the high points of any President's term of office' – it is known to have more protocol, more formality, but more splendour and magic than any other official trip abroad, and they expect it to be highly memorable. Another president, Nicolas Sarkozy of France, dined at Windsor in 2008. Bedevilled at home by a reputation for tasteless ostentation, his visit to the Queen was seen by the French media as a litmus-test of his gravitas. If he could pass muster on this occasion, it was implied, he might gain greater respect at home. In the event, he succeeded. The Queen presented him with a stamp album and they talked about this hobby, for her grandfather had also been an enthusiast. Where she has some common ground with a guest, she will make the most of it. How she coped with a visit from Nicolae Ceausescu of Romania and his wife (they came in 1978. He awarded her the Order of Socialist Romania), one cannot imagine, but with a far more welcome visitor, President Reagan, she went riding in Windsor Great Park. (An American photographer, lining up a shot, said to a Household official: 'Tell the Queen to get closer to Reagan!' and received the stiff rejoinder: 'One does not *tell* Her Majesty to do anything!')

Perhaps to her own surprise as much as anyone else's, the Queen was described as a 'fashion icon' while on a visit to Rome in 2002. Of course she is dressed by great designers, but only British ones, and with a deliberate avoidance of the quirks of fashion. Yet the clothing that appeals to other women is sometimes not her official costume but the practical, everyday garments she wears when off duty – these, after all, are not only comfortable and practical but comparatively affordable and easy to obtain. In Stephen Frears' 2006 film *The Queen*, much of the story is set at Balmoral. Her Majesty, as portrayed on the screen, dresses in the outdoor garments appropriate for a Scottish autumn. A world away from Deeside, amid the sophistication of Manhattan, shoppers wanted this same look. The *Daily Telegraph* announced that the film had caused a run on the Barbour jacket: 'New Yorkers want to dress like the Queen,' announced the paper, 'or, to be precise, they want to dress like Helen Mirren playing the Queen.' The manageress of the company's outlet was quoted as explaining: 'The first thing [customers] say is: "Have you seen *The Queen*?" Then they say they want the jacket that the Queen is wearing.' The Beaufort, one of several variations on the classic Barbour design, was the one in question. The very ordinariness of Her Majesty's everyday wardrobe is without doubt a means by which other women can identify with her. One, viewing the film at a London cinema, was heard to exclaim: '*I* have a dressing-gown just like that!'

Her handbags are much commented upon. She apparently has about 200 of them, which is not surprising in view of the range of outfits she possesses. Whatever she keeps in them it is not money, or a credit card, or a passport. One thing she does carry is an S-shaped hook – the sort one sees in butchers' shops – for hanging her bag on the edge of a table when she is dining. She will also have glasses, a fountain pen and a make-up case that was a gift to her from her husband when they married. Perhaps she has, in addition, family photographs and keys. She is said also to have crosswords cut out of newspapers, to beguile the time for a few minutes between engagements, and a notebook with information about people she is to meet.

Royal observers have noticed a code of signals with her handbag that tell her entourage what her reactions are. The bag on her left arm, with her gloves held in her right hand, is said to indicate that she is happy with proceedings. If she places the bag on the floor during a dinner it is a signal that she is bored by her companion and should be rescued. When stopping to talk to someone during a visit, she will drop the bag to one side to indicate that she is going to move on.

And the Royal Family too has moved on. Prince Charles appeared in public with Mrs Parker Bowles for the first time in 1999. Six years later the couple were married in a civil cere-mony at Windsor, and the Queen attended. The next genera-tion have, despite a certain amount of traditional grooming, had the chance to make their own way. Her grandsons William and Harry both took jobs in the Army that were demanding and dangerous and in which their royal status, far from helping them, has been a liability. Both have thus gained the respect of a public that continues to be resentful of privilege. William has, in any case, been far more free to live a normal life than any of those who preceded him as heir to the throne. Earning his way into university and in the Services, he has lived in anonymous flats, washed his own dishes, ordered take-aways, browsed in supermarkets, queued at cashpoints and walked the streets unrecognised, clad in the everlasting, jeans-and-trainers uniform of youth. When younger, he was more often photographed in sweatshirts than in a suit. William's courtship has been in keeping with this spirit of egalitarianism. He met a young woman just as any other student might have done. Once married, he even postponed his honeymoon through having to return to work. There has been no matchmaking, no vetting, no audible disapproval from any 'old guard' of courtiers. His experience has been significantly different from his father's, let alone that of his grandparents.

The Queen, who granted permission for him to marry, is aware of how this new generation of royalty fits the spirit of the times. Although his choice of wife has been dictated entirely by affection, it reflects the pattern in monarchies throughout Europe. In this bourgeois age, in which power is in the hands not of aristocrats but of businessmen, Royal Families have allied themselves with the middle class. Young members of the Royal Houses of Spain, Norway, Denmark and the Netherlands have without exception married people who work for a living. Royalty owes its survival to an ability to adapt, to reinvent itself, to remain old-fashioned without being left behind. As Princess Margaret once shrewdly observed: 'We can fit in with life as it is lived in our country at any given moment in time.'

Fifty years ago the Royal Family was described, by Malcolm Muggeridge, as being 'like a soap opera'. This is as true as ever – the comment has been made innumerable times since – and it is by no means necessarily a term of abuse.

Soap operas are hugely popular. Their fans number in the millions. People empathise with, sympathise with and emulate the characters. The public does not like the fictitious families to be too perfect, or always happy and successful. There must be tension, conflict and weakness in order to add excitement and keep blandness and boredom at bay. The plots must contain familiar elements without becoming tediously predictable. Where there are crises to overcome and problems to solve, viewers are assured that the lives they see on the screen are much like their own – or perhaps worse, which encourages a feeling of relieved complacency. Like any soap opera, old characters depart and new ones are introduced. In Windsor, as in Walford, children grow up, problems are resolved, disasters are averted or survived, and the story continues. There are financial crises, generational differences and tragic deaths. It is not, in fact, that the Royal Family is like a soap opera but that a soap opera is like *them*. Theirs is the story of all of us, writ large. They are what we would like to be, or perhaps don't want to be, but they are a mirror-image of us. The ups and downs of the Royal Family ensure interest. If there were no interest, they would be in danger of extinction.

Despite her age the Queen continues to be busier than anyone her years should expect to be, and is actually becoming more so. In 2010 she carried out 444 official engagements, of which 57 were overseas. In 2011, because of her grandson's wedding and her husband's 90th birthday, her diary was even fuller. Her historic visit to the Irish Republic in May served to underline both her personal magnetism and her continuing value as a symbol of goodwill. When she laid a wreath at a memorial to Irish patriots, her hosts were deeply touched. 'All Ireland missed a heartbeat,' reported the *Irish Independent*, 'when they saw her take a step back and bow her head.' She won more respect for beginning a speech with some words in gaelic. Those who met her described Her Majesty as 'full of life, full of fun', and a young woman gushed, with regard to the Queen and the Duke, that 'for their age, they're really bubbly and chatty'. Her gestures will have been premeditated and her speeches written for her, but the making of them was what counted, and by showing a warm, spontaneous nature during less formal moments, she added a further dimension to Anglo-Irish relations. 'Britain's ultimate diplomatic weapon' indeed.

In July 2009, Her Majesty – like her father King George and her great-grandmother Victoria – instituted a medal bearing her name. The Elizabeth Cross is not, like the others, an award for gallantry. It is not given to those who perform heroic deeds but to those – and there are sadly a great many of them – whose next of kin have been killed on operations or by acts of terrorism. Perhaps the biggest class of recipients will be the wives of servicemen, and the design is therefore distinctly feminine. A brooch rather than a medal, it has no ribbon and is modest in size. It will prove a highly suitable monument to a reign that has witnessed such tragedy in Northern Ireland, the Middle East and Afghanistan.

The Queen's own death is something she has always contemplated with equanimity. Devout in her Christian beliefs, she has no qualms about passing on to what Victoria called 'a more equal world', though as Alan Bennett has her remark in his play *An Englishman Abroad*: 'I suppose, for someone like me, heaven will be a bit of a come-down.' Plans for her eventual funeral have been in readiness ever since she came to the throne, though this is standard for all senior royals. They are updated annually by a committee, and known by the code-name 'London Bridge'. (The Queen Mother's funeral arrangements were 'Tay Bridge', and Prince Philip's are 'Forth Bridge'.) Once approved by this, the details are sent to the groups that would be affected: the City of Westminster, the Ministry of Defence and, naturally, the police. This is necessary because of what would be involved: the inviting of Heads of State from all over the world, the need to accommodate the international media, the deployment of troops and the closing off of parts of central London. The Queen's executors need not worry over where she will be buried or what the inscription on her tomb will say. All of that has long-since been settled. She has chosen her coffin, and apparently took great pleasure in fine-tuning the arrangements. It is a curious fact that Royals often do enjoy planning their own funerals. Lord Mountbatten had worked out in exhaustive detail how his was to be conducted.

When the Queen's funeral actually takes place – when 'London Bridge' is put into effect – the outpouring of affection will be massive. It will be on a scale not witnessed in Britain since the death of Victoria, and – since we are a more emotional people than the late-Victorians – probably greater. It will be a bigger event than anything in more recent times except, perhaps, the funeral of Gandhi.

When King George VI died the Prime Minister, Winston Churchill, laid a wreath on which were the simple words: 'For Valour'. This is the motto engraved on the Victoria Cross. For the King's daughter, whose overwhelming personal attribute has been undaunted, persistent personal courage, no lesser tribute would do.

Is Elizabeth II the best monarch Britain has ever had? It is difficult to say, for such a judgement must be conditional. There have been others who fitted the spirit of their age and who displayed the qualities necessary to lead the country through difficult or even catastrophic times. There is, in any case, no British Mount Rushmore on which the best few are represented. It is something of a cheap journalistic trick to say that the Queen's reign has been one of 'unprecedented change', for there is no era in modern history that has seen anything *other* than furious, ceaseless change, and contemporaries no doubt always thought of this as 'unprecedented'. What cannot be denied is that since the Second World War, Britain's position as a great power has collapsed with the loss of Empire and the shrinking of its ability to influence world affairs. This has meant that, to an extent no one could have foreseen, the burden of maintaining national prestige has fallen upon her shoulders. She has succeeded in carrying that burden for 60 years without making a single error, and that is a monumental attainment. Her calming influence, her tact and wisdom, her ability to make friends for Britain and to preside over the Commonwealth (an organisation that would almost certainly not still exist were it not for her devotion) have gained for her, and by extension her country, a continuing status. For the country this will rise and fall according to circumstance. For Queen Elizabeth it is something that time is very unlikely to erode. She has been blessed by Fortune with a temperament suited to her unique role, a series of good advisors, a supportive husband who has made his own contribution to history, and a reign that has lasted long enough for her to build great achievements. By any yardstick, and in any aspect of her life and work, she is a truly great figure, and those of us who are her subjects will always have good reason to be thankful that we have been New Elizabethans. The moment it has ended, her reign will be seen as a golden age – a time of stability and prosperity and creativity. Rather from awaiting that signal for an outburst of nostalgia, we would be wise to appreciate now the time in which we live.

# FURTHER READING

Bradford, Sarah – *Elizabeth*, QPD (Quality Paperbacks Direct), London, 1996

Colville, John – *The New Elizabethans, 1952–1977*, William Collins, 1977

Clark, Brigadier Stanley, OBE – *Palace Diary*, Geo. Harrap, 1958

Crawford, Marion – *Happy and Glorious*, George Newnes, 1953

Crawford, Marion – *The Little Princesses*, Cassell & Co., 1950

Dimbleby, Jonathan – *The Prince of Wales*, Little, Brown & Co., 1994

Duncan, Andrew – *The Reality of Monarchy*, William Heinemann, 1970

Edwards, Anne – *The Queen's Clothes*, Express/Elm Tree Books, 1976

Fisher, Graham and Heather – *The Queen's Life*, Robert Hale, 1976

Hall, Unity – *Philip: The Man Behind the Monarchy*, Michael O'Mara Books, 1987

Harris, Leonard – *Long to Reign Over Us?*, William Kimber, 1966

Harris, Marion – *The Queen's Windsor*, The Kensal Press, 1985

Hoey, Brian – *The Royal Yacht Britannia*, Patrick Stephens Ltd, 1995

Hoey, Brian – *Her Majesty: Fifty Regal Years*, Harper Collins, 2002

Jay, Antony – *Elizabeth R.*, BBC Books, 1992

Kenny, Mary – *Crown and Shamrock*, New Island, Ireland, 2009

Kiggell, Marcus, and Blakeway, Denys – *The Queen's Story*, Headline, 2002

Longford, Elizabeth – *Elizabeth R.*, Weidenfeld & Nicholson, 1983

Morrah, Dermot – *The Work of the Queen*, William Kimber, 1958

Nickolls, L.A. – *The Queen's Majesty*, Macmillan, 1957

Noakes, Michael & Vivien – *The Daily Life of the Queen*, Ebury Press, 2000

Oakey, David – *The Queen's Year: A Souvenir Album*, Royal Collection Publications, 2010

Piggott, Peter – *Royal Transport*, The Dundrun Group, Toronto, 2005

Pimlott, Ben – *The Queen: A Biography of Elizabeth II*, John Wiley & Sons, 1997

Prokashka, Frank – *The Eagle and the Crown: Americans and the British Monarchy*, Yale University Press, 2008

*The Royal Tour: A Souvenir Album*, Royal Collection Publications, 2009

Shawcross, William – *Queen Elizabeth, The Queen Mother: The Official Biography*, Macmillan, 2009

Whiting, Audrey – *Family Royal*, W. H. Allen, 1982

# INDEX